COUP/CLUCKS

BY JANE MARTIN

DRAMATISTS
PLAY SERVICE
INC.

COUP/CLUCKS
Copyright © 1982, 1984, Alexander Speer,
as Trustee for Jane Martin

All Rights Reserved

SPECIAL NOTE

COUP/CLUCKS was first presented by the Actors Theatre of Louisville, in Louisville, Kentucky, in November, 1982. It was directed by Jon Jory; the set design was by Paul Owen; costume design was by Karen Gerson; lighting design was by Jeff Hill; and the sound design by Mollysue Wedding. The cast, in order of appearance, was as follows:

COUP

MIZ ZIFTY	Jen Jones
DON	William Mesnik
BEULAH	Beatrice Winde
BRENDA LEE	Dawn Didawick
TOOTH	Dierk Torsek
ESSIE	Jessie K. Jones
BOBBY JOE	Daniel Jenkins
DR. KENNEDY	Reuben Green

CLUCKS

TRAVIS	Murphy Guyer
TOOTH	Dierk Torsek
BOBBY JOE	Daniel Jenkins
PRITCHARD	Ray Fry
RYMAN	William Mesnik
ZITS	John Short
DR. KENNEDY	Reuben Green
ESSIE	Jessie K. Jones

CONTENTS

COUP . . . . Page 5

CLUCKS . . . . Page 38

COUP

BY JANE MARTIN

COUP

*The play takes place in the living room of Miz Zifty's home, on
the morning of July 4th, in the small town of Brine, Alabama.
The set is realistic in that it represents accurately, if sparely, a
Victorian room in a home built at the end of the last century. It
is expressionistic in the sense that architectural detail is selective
and all of it, floor, ceiling, and walls, is white. The furniture,
a melange of French and English antiques, is white as well.
The properties, even the flowers, share this absence of color. The
costumes, however, provide bright accents and are, when de-
manded, exact copies of their counterparts in the film version of
"Gone With The Wind."*

*The lights reveal Miz Zifty, a woman in her mid- to late-sixties,
dressed in Scarlett O'Hara's green-flowered, white-muslin
party-dress. Miz Zifty is the social lion of this small world and
is preparing for her annual appearance in the Tara Parade and
Ball. Behind her, Don Savanah, a man in his early thirties,
arranges her hair. Born in Brine, he fled to New York only to be
drawn back to the South when his mother died. He is nattily
dressed with considerably more flair than is considered correct
locally. His manner is an odd combination of simple straight-
forwardness and an extroverted flamboyance. He is no fool.*

DON. (*Working on Miz Zifty's hair.*) Why did I come back to
Brine, Alabama? Leave the bright lights of New York City?
Cowardice, I suppose. I swear, wherever I go I feel like a fly in
a frogpond. Victim-in-residence. They ever made a movie about
me they'd call it "Born to Shake." Makes me just furious I can't
change my nature. Know who I'm comin' back as in my next
life? John Wayne. (*Handing her a mirror.*) Here, peek.
MIZ ZIFTY. (*Doubtfully.*) Well . . .
DON. Darlin', you're the personification, that's what you are.
MIZ ZIFTY. You'd think the very least the Good Lord could
have done would have been to make old age pretty.

7

DON. Oh, poo. If Ashley Wilkes doesn't nibble you like a pra-line, the man's a stone. So, anyway, I'd quit my hair stylin' job 'cause I was petrified to take the subway, and there I was, cata-tonic in Times Square, appalled by the sheer unendurable ugli-ness, transfixed by the lack, the absence of any beauty, anything soothing to the soul, when suddenly I was struck from behind . . . hard enough to see stars. I turn, and there is a wild man, a Martian savage dressed entirely in debris. Had on plastic Chlorox bottles for shoes, white garbage bags wrapped for leg-gin's, cardboard mailing tubes on his arms, face caked with filth, plus he had on, so help me Hannah, an actual Medieval breastplate. Like out of a museum, darlin'. And this staff he struck me with is covered with "Nixon's The One" buttons. Well, his wild blue eyes lock with mine, he grabs my Pierre Cardin tie, shakes me like a rag doll and shrieks in my face, "Why don't you weirdos get the hell out of New York City!"

MIZ ZIFTY. That doesn't surprise you, I hope. That's normal Yankee behavior. (*Beulah, Miz Zifty's sixty-year-old black maid, enters carrying a tray which holds several bowls of finger-foods. She places them about the room.*)

DON. Well, I fled, darlin', fled home to Brine. Our rednecks may be mean, dumb and violent, but at least they are not dressed in Medieval breastplates. You seen 'em out on the square this mornin'? Waitin' t' laugh y'all to shame?

MIZ ZIFTY. Primitive barbarians, ought to be moved on with a cattle prod.

BEULAH. Here, here!

DON. (*Stands back to look at Miz Zifty.*) Well, I guess that just about dots the 'i'.

MIZ ZIFTY. I was not raised to be intimidated by white trash.

DON. There.

MIZ ZIFTY. My twenty-third annual and consecutive year as Scarlett O'Hara.

BEULAH. Huh! (*She exits into the kitchen.*)

MIZ ZIFTY. Heroine of the South. Flower of a lost civilization. You know that Coretta whatever, the one who wears purple paisley dresses with pink cowboy-boots?

DON. You mean Coretta's Beauty Nook, last bastion of the concrete beehive hairdo? Miss Hands-of-Stone?

MIZ ZIFTY. Yes, *that* one. Came to a D.A.C. meetin' uninvited and suggested we replace the Tara Parade and Ball with a greased-pig mud-grab and a donkey baseball celebrity-night game. Said that would really get the community *involved*.

DON. Well she's just perfect for donkey baseball. Course when you were ridin' her your hands would get stuck in her hairspray.

MIZ ZIFTY. The Tara Parade is Brine, Alabama's cultural Alamo and it will become a donkey baseball game over my shot dead body.

DON. Well, I admire your raw nerve but those cromagnons out there . . . Lord have mercy!

MIZ ZIFTY. Just the wiff of fear and they sting like honeybees.

DON. (*He shivers.*) Pick-ups, crossed eyes, shot-guns an' buck-knives.

MIZ ZIFTY. All you boys of good family gone soft as fudge candy. Where is the Southern elite with the barbarians at the gate? All gone to Hilton Head, that's where. Scaredycats. In ancient Sparta young boys would allow the foxes held under their tunics to eat away their vitals rather than show a shred of pain. Courage is a made quality, not a born one. See here? (*She lifts her sleeve to show a safety-pin pinned through the flesh of her upper arm. Beulah enters, carrying a feather-duster, with which she proceeds to dust various objects.*)

DON. My God, there's a safety pin clipped through your flesh!

BEULAH. Ain't the only one either. Some nights she looks like a tailor mark her for alterations.

MIZ ZIFTY. Pain doesn't bother me. I like it. I'm vaccinated against it. When called upon to suffer I'll be prepared.

DON. You may be a small-town girl, darlin', but you've got a real future in a New-Wave band.

MIZ ZIFTY. Scarlett O'Hara suffered, and I *am* Scarlett O'Hara. (*Turning in dress.*) Well, do I pass muster?

DON. Darlin', you got her down in spades.

BEULAH. Who you callin' a spade?

DON. Oh shush.

MIZ ZIFTY. That is a piquant homily, Beulah, and not a racial slur.

BEULAH. Well, I got a pecan homily says you're too damn old t' go gettin' doxied-up like a Southern Belle.

MIZ ZIFTY. Great ballerinas play young girls well into their maturity.

9

BEULAH. You mean thirty-five maturity or sixty-five maturity?
DON. Well aren't we a prickly little pear today?
BEULAH. An' you're still a big ol' fruit. (*She exits into the kitchen.*)
MIZ ZIFTY. I will not have squibble-squabblin', y'all hear me?
After the parade I don't care a hate if the two of you beat each
other to doll-rags, but right now I want . . . no, I insist . . . on
harmony. (*Looking at the back of her dress.*) Am I ridin' too low?
DON. Just billows right over your hoops.
BEULAH. (*Entering, still puttering and muttering.*) Fourth of July
in the wax museum.
MIZ ZIFTY. Now remember, best port glasses when we come
back for refreshments after the parade, and most important, the
place cards must correspond to the flower-favors handed out as
the guests arrive.
BEULAH. (*Heading for kitchen and exiting.*) Whole lot of damn
trouble for one damn glass of wine.
DON. (*To Miz Zifty.*) Here, slip on these green, flat-heeled,
morocco slippers. (*He kneels down to help her.*)
MIZ ZIFTY. I just love your new touches.
DON. Why you keep such ill-tempered help I'll never know.
MIZ ZIFTY. She was given to me as a personal maid by
Mother on my wedding day and she's been with me ever since.
It is only irresponsible Yankees who change their servants on a
whim.
DON. They're so rude up there they don't even smile when
you're makin' love to 'em.
MIZ ZIFTY. My great-uncle, Attila Zifty, contended that all
Yankees suffer a derangement of the blood brought on by
drinkin' inferior bourbon, ridin' lop-gaited horses, and listenin'
to German-born opera singers until they became mad as hat-
ters. Well, I do hope Melda is sending over Bobby Joe with my
cinch and sashed-straw.
DON. Thank God Southern girls are still taught to sew. Well,
it's just a cryin' shame you don't have a Rhett Butler with real
panache.
MIZ ZIFTY. I inquired after your availability.
DON. No, I don't think those "HeeHaw" regulars out there are
ready for me.
MIZ ZIFTY. In any case, Travis Scroggins, however unwill-
ingly, has escorted me at both the Tara Parade and Ball for five

years, and there is no disputing he's a ringer for Mr. Gable.

DON. Oh, he was my idol in high school. Only boy could crush beer cans with his teeth. If I'd been more sure of myself, I would have invited him to the prom.

MIZ ZIFTY. With so many leaving town for Houston, we are fortunate to have any Rhett Butler at all. (*Beulah returns with a rubber plant. She crosses to the front door and places the plant outside.*) You have the oleanders out, Beulah?

BEULAH. (*Returning.*) Uh-huh, and the hydrangeas, geraniums, coleaus, magnolias, pink-crepe myrtle, and those four damn rubber plants you had sent over from the florist.

MIZ ZIFTY. All flowers they had at antebellum balls. Now, you remember to remind any young ladies who do not realize that married women sit separately, to go 'round to the screen porch.

BEULAH. These cats 'round here always find the right wall. (*She goes out to the kitchen.*)

MIZ ZIFTY. Honestly. Will you be goin' as Rene Picard again Don?

DON. I don't dare the parade, but I wouldn't miss the ball. It's a teensie part in the movie, but it's worth it to dress as a Louisiana Zouave. (*The doorbell rings.*) Good heavens, I'm not even dressed.

MIZ ZIFTY. Well, I'm dyin' to see, so you go on.

DON. You're sure?

MIZ ZIFTY. I believe my mother trained me to deal with early arrivals. You perfectly positive you won't parade? (*Beulah enters to answer the doorbell.*)

DON. Maybe when I put it on I'll find my courage like the Cowardly Lion. (*He exits.*)

BEULAH. (*Ushers in Brenda Lee and Tooth. Brenda Lee is an odd combination of belle and tough cookie. He is a redneck once-removed. She is dressed as Melanie in gray organdy, and he is resplendent as Ashley Wilkes.*) Here's some more nuts for your nut mix. (*Beulah exits back to the kitchen.*)

BRENDA LEE. Lord, it's so hot out there I'm gettin' mascara down my cleavage! Oooooooo, I just *hate* walkin' by those boys in the square.

TOOTH. Ol' Dim Danny dropped a quarter down her boobies.

BRENDA LEE. (*Hitting him.*) You be quiet. (*Goes to Miz Zifty.*)

11

Golly gee, you just look good enough to eat! Will you look at this? Just scrumptious, I swear. (*To Tooth.*) Don't she just put Vivien Leigh to shame!

TOOTH. (*Tipping his hat.*) How you doin' Miz Zifty?

MIZ ZIFTY. (*Curtsying.*) Mr. Ashley Wilkes, I do believe.

BRENDA LEE. Said he wasn't goin' to parade today, but I jes' told him if that was the case he could kiss his nighttime privileges goodbye. Buy him a duck or a Barbie Doll, the ol' poop. (*Hits him. Goes to Miz Zifty.*) I'm just lovin' that flowered muslin. Jes' how many yards did that take?

MIZ ZIFTY. Scarlett's original took twelve yards, but this took somewhat more.

BRENDA LEE. No such thing. Looks like she got a seventeen-inch waist, don't it Tooth?

TOOTH. You bet. Where's Travis?

MIZ ZIFTY. Mr. Scroggins has not as yet made his annual appearance.

BRENDA LEE. Just scared to death he'll hafta go out there alone.

TOOTH. What he was drinkin' last night I sure hope he makes it. Went through four cases of beer.

BRENDA LEE. Shush up y' ol' redneck! (*Hits him.*) I honestly don't know how a nice Southern deb like myself ended up with a dirt farmer like you.

TOOTH. Probably 'cause you stuck yer hands in my pants.

BRENDA LEE. Now you just hush! These men have already been out playin' softball, hog-callin', drinkin' beer an' heaven knows what else, an' it's not even twelve noon.

TOOTH. Man don't get drunk on July fourth ain't patriotic. Tell you one thing. Way it is out there now Miz Zifty, come the parade yer gonna sweat fierce.

BRENDA LEE. Southern gentlemen don't say sweat.

TOOTH. What they say?

BRENDA LEE. Dew or dewey.

TOOTH. (*To Miz Zifty.*) Well then, you two'll git dewey and I'll jes' sweat my butt off.

BRENDA LEE. (*To Miz Zifty.*) Essie says y'all are goin' to say lines this year.

MIZ ZIFTY. Well, it was Mr. Savanah's idea really.

TOOTH. (*Snorting.*) Mr. Savanah!

BRENDA LEE. At the band shell?

MIZ ZIFTY. That is correct. The parade will pause briefly in the park and Mr. Scroggins and myself will represent the passage where Rhett Butler wagers Scarlett a box of bon-bons against a kiss that the Yankees will take Atlanta.

BRENDA LEE. Excitin'! You know Essie's been drillin' Travis on those lines since Christmas, but I don't know . . .

MIZ ZIFTY. In case of a lapse of memory, I will prevail upon Mr. Savanah to prompt.

TOOTH. He ain't Mr. Savanah. He is plain ol' Don Snots.

BRENDA LEE. You were just little boys then.

TOOTH. Yeah, an' some of us grew up to be big boys, an' some of us went to New Yawk an' turned into somethin' else entirely.

BRENDA LEE. Don Savanah is a marvelous name for a hairdresser.

TOOTH. Guess you ladies just didn't want somebody named Snot gittin' his hands in your hair.

BRENDA LEE. I swear sometimes you just have the raisin' of a hog.

TOOTH. You know what downhill is? All the good ol' boys leave for Texas, an' the only folks movin' in is a colored dentist and a hairdressin' fairy.

MIZ ZIFTY. We do not use that word in the South, young man, ever. Mr. Savanah is simply a perennial bachelor.

TOOTH. Well it gives me the willies, shakin' his hand. Feels like Teflon.

MIZ ZIFTY. I prefer that a man not have the skin of a rhinocerous.

TOOTH. No matter what I got on, he says it oughta be took-in in the back.

MIZ ZIFTY. Mr. Savanah is sensitive to apparel. He is the official costumiere for the Tara Ball.

TOOTH. Well, he's just a tad too interested in my back-seam.

BRENDA LEE. Honey, he flies down to Birmingham on the weekends for his social needs. Now I don't want to hear any more rough talk. (*Don reappears as a Louisiana Zouave, wearing a red jacket and baggy, blue-and-white striped pants.*)

DON. Voilá!

BRENDA LEE. Now that's cute!

13

DON. "Respectable? All my days I was respectable until ze war set me free lak ze darkies. . . ."
BRENDA LEE. So cute!
DON. "Never again must I be deegnified and full of ennui. Lak Napolean I follow my star!" (*Brenda applauds.*) God, don't you just love "Gone With The Wind"!
BRENDA LEE. *Love it!*
DON. Lord, I've seen that movie nine times in a week.
BRENDA LEE. Ain't he just slick as a baby's bottom?
MIZ ZIFTY. Absolutely perfect.
DON. (*Looking briefly at Tooth.*) Those trousers look like they need to be taken up in the back.
TOOTH. I like to wear 'em loose, Horse. (*Don turns to Brenda Lee.*)
DON. Well, don't we just look like peaches-and-cream!
BRENDA LEE. Don't think I don't know why y'all picked me for *this* part.
MIZ ZIFTY. Because the sweet, gray satin and accordian-petal pleating set off your coloring, dear.
BRENDA LEE. 'Cause in the book Melanie is jes' plain as ol' dishwater.
MIZ ZIFTY. It also speaks of creamy skin, and brown eyes that have the still gleam of a forest-pool in winter, when brown leaves shine up through quiet water.
BRENDA LEE. Honey, rotten leaves don't constitute no compliment to me. What's happenin' to me is the worst thing can happen to a corn-fed, all-American, cheerleader-type like me. I'm losin' the cutes. Cain't bounce up and down and squeal no more, cain't risk a giggle, an' a pony-tail makes me look like Trigger. Tooth Gannet, can you honestly stare me right in my brown eyes an' tell me I'm cute?
TOOTH. Well, no.
BRENDA LEE. See?
TOOTH. But yer lookin' a whole lot more like Joanne Woodward.
BRENDA LEE. Joanne Woodward is fifty-years-old! I can't go out in the Tara Parade lookin' like Joanne Woodward!
DON. Now honey, Joanne Woodward *smoulders.*
BRENDA LEE. I ain't your honey, I don't care to smoulder, an' I wanna be cute! (*Beulah enters, bringing a coffee service.*)

14

DON. Missy, when the fire banks low is when the coals git *hot*.
BRENDA LEE. (*Suspicious*.) Really?
DON. You on a direct flight from cute to sexy.
BRENDA LEE. You mean it?
DON. Cross my heart.
BRENDA LEE. You ain't jes' sweet-teasin'?
DON. Wanna go out to the drive-in an' go all the way?
BRENDA LEE. (*Punching his arm*.) Y'ol' cute thing! Well,
thank-goodness, thank-double-goodness! Sexy is more eighties
anyway. Don't you think? I think so. Maybe I'll have this cut
lower next year. Lordy, don't you love dressin' up? Three cheers
for the Tara Parade. Rescues at least one day from the ugly
present. (*Gunshots outside*.) What on earth is that?
TOOTH. Boys is gittin' restless.
BRENDA LEE. Those boys *loved* cute. I hope "sexy" don't git
'em too riled-up.
MIZ ZIFTY. My father trained me to face that rabble down.
BRENDA LEE. Such a tiresome, ugly ol' world out there. I
swear there's nothing left but make-believe. Scarlett O'Hara,
dancin', twinkle-lights, all of us singin' "Bonnie Blue Flag."
There can't have been anything as beautiful in all history as the
Ol' South before the Yankees came an' broke it.
MIZ ZIFTY. There are a few precious moments in history
when culture, breedin', an' imagination combine to create, for
split seconds, an earthly paradise, an' our Cotton Kingdom was
one. (*Beulah applauds. They turn to look at her*.)
BEULAH. How about the slaves?
DON. Oh, hush-up!
BEULAH. They git in on this-here paradise?
MIZ ZIFTY. We do not wish, once again, to hear about the
slaves at this time.
BEULAH. Yo' grandaddy had him three hundred in *his* earthly
paradise.
MIZ ZIFTY. Slavery was simply the system of welfare benefits
of that time.
BEULAH. An' what was floggin'?
MIZ ZIFTY. We never flogged, we spanked.
BEULAH. An' your grandaddy shootin' my grandaddy?
MIZ ZIFTY. A dreadful mistake for which my family has for
always and ever been tryin' to make up to your family, which is

15

precisely, as you very well know, the reason I bought you in the first place . . . I mean hired you.

BEULAH. You know what I do with you in my dreams? I eat you with barbecue-sauce. (*She exits back to the kitchen.*)

TOOTH. How come you let that old woman talk to you like that in your own house?

MIZ ZIFTY. Because she is the single, last, black domestic in this town and must be treated with all the rights and privileges of an endangered species.

BRENDA LEE. Well I swear, I'd rather do for myself! Shoot, I'd fix my own dinner if somebody'd teach me.

MIZ ZIFTY. Now that is precisely the mistake your generation makes, if I must say so. Doin' for yourself causes the terrible frustration, loneliness, and agitation of spirit that leads you straight down the primrose path to Yankee feminism. I guarantee you that ninety-percent of the problems in any marriage could be solved by a live-in maid.

BRENDA LEE. (*To Tooth.*) You listenin' to this, Tooth?

TOOTH. Where the hell am I going to get a live-in maid?

DON. Name a price.

TOOTH. Over my dead body.

DON. Ooooooo, kinky.

TOOTH. Now you knock that off!

ESSIE. (*Off-stage voice.*) Miz Zifty?

MIZ ZIFTY. In here dear. (*Essie enters. She is the wife of Travis who was to play Rhett Butler. She is Brenda Lee's best friend. Currently she is dressed as Mammy, Scarlett's servant in "Gone With The Wind," bandanna, black-face and all.*)

ESSIE. Well, I'm afraid we have just a peck of *trouble*.

MIZ ZIFTY. God's nightgown! Who are you?

BRENDA LEE. Jimminy Cricket!

ESSIE. I'm Essie.

BRENDA LEE. ESSIE!

ESSIE. Well goodness, surely you can recognize my voice?

BRENDA LEE. That's not Essie.

ESSIE. Lord's sake, Brenda Lee!

BRENDA LEE. How old was I when I lost my virginity?

ESSIE. Eighth grade on the class hayride.

BRENDA LEE. Lord, it *is* Essie!

TOOTH. Travis see you got up like that?

ESSIE. Mr. Travis Scroggins does not dictate the way I dress.

TOOTH. May not care how you dress, but he's pretty picky about your race.

BRENDA LEE. He musta' been mad as a mud-dauber!

ESSIE. Smoke comin' out of both ears.

BRENDA LEE. Did he hit himself like he does sometimes?

ESSIE. Blacked his own eye an' knocked the princess phone through the kitchen window.

BRENDA LEE. Well it's . . .

MIZ ZIFTY. (*Taking charge.*) Get yourself home and scrub your face!

ESSIE. It is time for a change and I *won't*.

MIZ ZIFTY. *This* is no change, young woman, it is a calamity!

ESSIE. Well, it's hateful injustice that there are no black characters represented at the Tara Parade and Ball.

MIZ ZIFTY. They are minor characters.

BRENDA LEE. Plus colored people don't waltz.

ESSIE. Great heavens, they are not invisible. They are there. They are in the book. They are black and they are in the book.

MIZ ZIFTY. I never notice them when I read it.

ESSIE. Well, you are gonna notice them today!

DON. Why don't you let me get you a Coke?

MIZ ZIFTY. I forbid you to parade in that outfit.

ESSIE. Mammy, Prissy, Park and Big Sam are just as important a part of "Gone With The Wind" as any white person.

MIZ ZIFTY. The Tara Ball, young woman, is not an *issue*. It is a charitable event.

ESSIE. To benefit the Daughters of the Confederacy, which has no black members.

MIZ ZIFTY. No colored person has ever made application.

ESSIE. And no lamb hands the lion a knife an' fork either!

MIZ ZIFTY. And in that inflammatory get-up you intend to dance the night away?

ESSIE. I can do the Virginia reel just as well black as white.

MIZ ZIFTY. And just who, pray tell, do you assume will partner you?

ESSIE. Some liberated gentleman who does not assume that race can be contracted like influenza.

MIZ ZIFTY. There is, thank heaven, no such person in Brine, Alabama!

DON. I'll dance with her.

ESSIE. Thank you! Thank you very much.

TOOTH. Sure. You two'll just be the couple of the year.

MIZ ZIFTY. I will not have twenty-three years of herculean labor against incalculable odds and philistine indifference flushed down the drain by a Northern-educated twit whose total misunderstanding of "Gone With The Wind" has parboiled her brain!

TOOTH. You sure your dental bills ain't gittin' too high?

BRENDA LEE. Oh my, oh my.

ESSIE. And just what exactly does that mean?

TOOTH. Nothin'. Jes' seen your car over to the dentist's.

ESSIE. It just so happens I am having my teeth capped. (*Beulah enters from the kitchen.*)

TOOTH. Sure you are.

ESSIE. I am!

TOOTH. Well, I just hope Travis leaves 'em in yer mouth.

ESSIE. (*Irate.*) You are awful, horrible, small-minded, bigoted people!

BEULAH. (*Loudly.*) What in hell you think you doin', white girl?

ESSIE. (*Caught off balance.*) Doin'?

BEULAH. You got about four seconds to git that impertinence off you, 'fore I come down on you like a duck on a june-bug.

ESSIE. Oh Beulah. . . .

BEULAH. What you think yer doin' get-up like some plantation nigger?

ESSIE. This is Mammy, Beulah. She's the most beautiful character in "Gone With The Wind."

BEULAH. Beautiful. There ain't no slave that's beautiful, Missy, an' there ain't no white woman alive on this planet gonna mock the pain of slavery long as I'm around.

ESSIE. I'm not mockin'. Oh Beulah, really, really I'm not.

BEULAH. I don't care if you make jack-ass fools out of yoselves, paradin' aroun' in your Johnny Reb, hand-me-down, slave-tradin', black-floggin', anti-bellum outfits, but there ain't gonna be no black-face minstrel show carryin' on in my town, an' you can count on that.

ESSIE. But I didn't mean. . . .

BEULAH. Ain't nobody in the South meant nothin' 'bout nothin' in two hundred years, but we still keep gettin' it in the

neck. Now you git that black shoe-polish offa your face or I'll
damn-well scrub it with a cheese-grater an' whitewash it like
a damn picket fence! (*Essie bursts into tears as Beulah exits to the
kitchen.*)
BRENDA LEE. Now look what you've done.
ESSIE. Everything I touch turns to cow-pies.
DON. (*Handing her a handkerchief.*) Here, use this.
ESSIE. I could just cry myself to sleep.
DON. Poor baby.
BRENDA LEE. Will someone explain to me why colored peo-
ple will not let us do one solitary thing for them? I mean,
for years they've wanted to be in the Tara Parade and now . . .
(*Pointing to Essie.*) We let one in and look what happens. (*Essie
breaks out sobbing again.*)
DON. (*Sitting Essie down.*) What you need is one of Don Sa-
vanah's imported-from-Paris lemon pastilles.
ESSIE. I *hate* lemon pastilles.
MIZ ZIFTY. *Now*, what we have to do is get you dressed as
India Wilkes as you were meant to be.
ESSIE. I can't.
BRENDA LEE. It's a scrumptious dress.
ESSIE. I just can't.
MIZ ZIFTY. Never say can't.
BRENDA LEE. Remember Little Toot?
ESSIE. Little Toot? (*Brenda Lee makes a train whistle sound.*)
BRENDA LEE. I *think* I can, I think I can, I think I can . . .
toot, toot . . . I know I can, I know I can, I know I can, I *will!*
(*Essie breaks out crying again.*)
TOOTH. I'm in a damn nut hutch!
BRENDA LEE. Great gollywhompers, it's eleven forty-five!
MIZ ZIFTY. Quarter-of?
BRENDA LEE. That's right.
MIZ ZIFTY. Lord have *mercy!* We're supposed to be formed up
behind the band at twelve. (*To Tooth.*) Go into the kitchen and
bring me some dish rags and Crisco. (*To Don.*) Run for your life
and bring this child the mustard-silk India Wilkes dress. In a
twinklin', you hear? Shoo! (*To Essie.*) You're sure to look so
glamorous in that silk dress you won't care what happens to colored people. Now where's your handsome husband, our es-
teemed Rhett Butler?

19

ESSIE. He won't.

MIZ ZIFTY. Won't what?

ESSIE. Won't be Rhett Butler.

MIZ ZIFTY. He is Rhett Butler.

ESSIE. Says he won't say no dumb lines, tired of his cronies laughin' at him, says he won't go out there with his wife playin' Aunt Jemima, and Rhett Butler is an asshole just like everybody else from Charleston.

MIZ ZIFTY. I happen to be from Charleston.

ESSIE. He says you're included. He also happens to be too dead drunk to walk.

TOOTH. (*Reappears from kitchen.*) Ol' Beulah won't give me the Crisco. Says it's for cookies, not nitwits.

DON. (*Returning with the dress.*) You're gonna look sensational, and I know 'cause I tried it on.

MIZ ZIFTY. (*To Essie.*) You march right on home and drag that ruffian back here by his ear.

ESSIE. It won't matter.

MIZ ZIFTY. Won't matter?

ESSIE. I already got someone else.

BRENDA LEE. For Rhett Butler?

ESSIE. Yes, I did.

MIZ ZIFTY. For the parade and the ball?

ESSIE. I just said that. Didn't I just say that?

DON. (*Undressing Essie.*) We'll just get you out of these rags . . . where's the Crisco?

TOOTH. I jes' told you she won't hand it over.

DON. (*Going to the kitchen.*) She will hand it over to me or I will expose myself.

MIZ ZIFTY. (*To Essie.*) The Daughters of the Confederacy offer these roles by majority vote.

ESSIE. Well, we only had an hour.

MIZ ZIFTY. I would have tendered the role to Judge Parseghian.

BRENDA LEE. Lord, he's three-sheets-gone in the nursin' home. Step out of this . . . (*To Essie.*) There isn't another single soul in this town could pass for Clark Gable at dusk with the light behind 'em. Jimmy John McLean?

ESSIE. Yuk.

MIZ ZIFTY. Colonel Carter?

ESSIE. Are you jokin'?

BRENDA LEE. Have you seen that man's teeth? I wouldn't touch him with a surgical sponge.

MIZ ZIFTY. Well who, for heaven's sake? Who?

DON. (*Enters with the Crisco and rags.*) Voilá, the Count of Monte Crisco!

BRENDA LEE. Oh, you got it. Good.

DON. I have shown our Beulah things no white woman has ever seen before.

BRENDA LEE. She's not white, sillykins.

DON. Well she is now. (*To Tooth.*) Fetch me a towel, will you Horse?

TOOTH. (*Going.*) I just can't picture this happenin' in Brine, Alabama.

DON. Is there a single soul here who gives two hoots for the Tara Parade?

MIZ ZIFTY. I am tryin' to find out . . .

DON. Because you are all standin' stock-still like shock victims and *time is passin'.*

MIZ ZIFTY. . . . who my Rhett Butler . . .

DON. At ten minutes to twelve it doesn't matter if it's Rin-Tin-Tin in a top hat! We have to hurry! Now there is just no time for your hair, Brenda Lee . . .

BRENDA LEE. But I want it cute . . .

DON. You will just have to . . .

BRENDA LEE. Fluffy. Fluffy and *cute!*

DON. . . . give it a lick and a spit curl . . .

BRENDA LEE. Oooooooooo, you make me so crazy . . .

DON. (*Bringing Miz Zifty over to her.*) And take the former Miss Magnolia of some undetermined pre-war year with you.

BRENDA LEE. (*Gathering her things.*) I could just throw a hissy!

DON. (*Pushing them out.*) And cinch her waist till her eyes pop an' she whistles "Dixie" out her ears.

MIZ ZIFTY. But Don darlin'!

BRENDA LEE. Cute, make it cute!

MIZ ZIFTY. Don . . .

DON. (*Closing the door on them.*) Out! (*Leaning on it.*) Lord have mercy!

ESSIE. I don't see how you could ever, ever, come back here from New York.

21

DON. (*Starting to clean her face with the Crisco.*) Home, darlin', is where, when you have to go there, they have to take you in.

ESSIE. Who said that?

DON. Every poor faggot who ever left Dixie.

ESSIE. You're so hard on yourself.

DON. Just old enough to eat the pancake plain, darlin'. Know what I was in New York? Wallpaper. Chopped liver. Nuthin' at all! When Momma died and left me the beauty shop, I just packed up my troubles in my ol' kit bag an' caught the Continental Trailways home.

ESSIE. But isn't it hard to be different?

DON. (*Smiling.*) Different? (*Gunshots outside.*)

ESSIE. (*Indicating outside.*) Don't they scare you?

DON. Honey, I'm panicky wherever I am, so I might as well be petrified where I can do the accent.

ESSIE. Well, it beats me down . . . I just want to show 'em . . . just once . . .

DON. (*Working on her face.*) Look over there.

ESSIE. It's like they build the ceilings so low here, it won't let you grow up. It's a physical pain to stop growing and know it. Don't you think so?

DON. I wouldn't know darlin'. I'm like Peter Pan. I don't want to grow up. (*Looking at her face.*) My God, you're white! I want you to have my babies!

ESSIE. (*Giggling.*) You stop it!

DON. Now, just a lick and a promise.

ESSIE. These people are starvin' to death on short rations of the mind. You know how, when you put a nice plump sausage patty in the pan an' it sizzles a little while, and comes out three times smaller? Well, Brine, Alabama is the pan.

DON. An' ol' Travis, the ex-Rhett?

ESSIE. Bein' fried away at an even faster rate. Such a King Moose when we were growin' up. Sexy as sin. You could lose your virginity just lookin' at him. First time he touched me it raised welts. You could see the shape of his hands in perfect red marks on my body. First Momma fainted an' then she sent me North for a year with Aunt Bettina. He had a mind, too, but where, oh where, has it gone? Gone like the water in the sausage.

DON. Well, if it's any consolation, there is damn few of us gettin' better. There. You're so clean the hogs wouldn't know you. (*Tooth enters with the towel.*)

TOOTH. Sorry. Had to make a pit stop.

DON. (*Taking the towel.*) Will you do one more thing for me?

TOOTH. Yeah, what?

DON. Take off all your clothes and pretend you're a gorilla?

TOOTH. You gonna get it, Horse. (*Brenda Lee re-enters with a comb and mirror.*)

DON. (*Hands Essie dress.*) Now, you put this on and pack up *your* troubles in a ol' kit bag.

BRENDA LEE. Will somebody do *somethin'* with this unmanageable mop on my head? I swear, it looks like garden mulch in a high wind.

DON. (*Turns to Brenda Lee.*) Melanie honey, I told you you're too old for cheap wigs. (*He fusses with her hair. Essie dresses.*)

BRENDA LEE. I got Miz Zifty laced an' cinched an' now she's decided on a two-minute cucumber facial.

DON. *Over* the rouge?

BRENDA LEE. Just around the eyes, to tighten up the laugh-lines.

DON. (*Still working on her hair.*) Honey, if those are laugh-lines, that woman's spent her whole life in hysterics.

ESSIE. Will you zip me up, Tooth?

TOOTH. (*Doubtfully.*) Well . . .

ESSIE. Good lord, Travis isn't here to eat you! (*He catches flesh in the zipper.*) Ow!

BRENDA LEE. Here, let me. (*To Tooth.*) Butterfingers!

DON. (*Looking at Tooth, appalled.*) Ashley Wilkes, do you call that a bow tie?

TOOTH. (*Backing away.*) Nosiree.

DON. (*Exasperated.*) Look. I am a human being, not the "Creature of the Black Lagoon." I am trying to improve your appearance, not your sex life. Now stand still, or I'll whip your ass. (*Don slaps him on the behind and Tooth is astounded enough to stand still as Don fixes his tie.*)

BRENDA LEE. (*Whispers to Essie.*) You jes' nervous as a pig on ice.

ESSIE. (*Guiltily.*) I am?

BRENDA LEE. Your Rhett Butler isn't who I think it is, is it?

(*Essie nods yes.*)

ESSIE. Well, maybe . . .

BRENDA LEE. My God, you're a lunatic.

ESSIE. Well, why not?

BRENDA LEE. Travis is gonna have a conniption.

ESSIE. Well, maybe it will wake him up.

BRENDA LEE. It'll turn his blood to Dr. Pepper.

DON. (*Finishing with Travis.*) Much better.

ESSIE. He jes' drills on my teeth an' talks.

TOOTH. (*Grudgingly.*) Thanks.

DON. Don't mention it.

ESSIE. He has an actual brain. (*The doorbell rings. Essie clutches her heart.*) Oh God.

BRENDA LEE. I can't staaaaaaaaand it! I can't. I'll throw up.

MIZ ZIFTY. (*Offstage.*) Would one of you girls get that? (*Beulah enters.*)

DON. I will.

BEULAH. You touch that door and you're a dead pale.

BRENDA LEE. I just can't staaaaaaaaand it!

BEULAH. Don't want nobody sayin' I'm not doin' *my* job. (*Goes to the door.*)

DON. (*A presentation.*) And now, from Charleston, the notorious blockade-runner, the ironic, disreputable, Rhett Butler! (*Beulah opens the door. Bobby Joe Bigun, a boy of seventeen, dressed in old jeans, a t-shirt and an Atlanta Braves baseball-cap, plus clod hoppers is revealed.*) Taa-daa!

BOBBY JOE. How y'all doin'?

BRENDA LEE. (*Relieved it wasn't who she thought.*) Thank God.

BEULAH. Bobby Joe Bigun, what you want?

BOBBY JOE. Melda sent me over with some stuff she sewed up for Miz Zifty.

DON. (*Struck.*) My God, you're like a Botticelli angel. Who are you?

BOBBY JOE. Bobby Joe Bigun, come on a delivery.

DON. Well you come right in here and take off your cap. (*Leads him in, and removes the cap.*) My dear, you're translucent!

ESSIE. Now Don . . .

BRENDA LEE. Bobby Joe? (*Doesn't answer. He stares open mouthed at Don.*) Bobby Joe?

BOBBY JOE. Huh?

24

BRENDA LEE. You don't close that mouth, you're gonna catch flies. (*Hits him.*) Whatcha got?

BOBBY JOE. Big straw-hat an' a waistcincher.

BRENDA LEE. Good!

DON. (*Almost moved to tears by the boy's voice.*) Big straw-hat an' a waistcincher!

ESSIE. Don . . .

BEULAH. Hand that stuff over. (*Bobby Joe does. A small band is heard striking up.*) Ol' Pritchard finally got there with his tuba, so ya'll better get a move on.

DON. (*Beulah takes the hat and cincher to Miz Zifty.*) Do you think any of us were ever that young once?

ESSIE. (*Putting a hand on Don's shoulder.*) You hush now.

DON. God, how I hate mortality!

BOBBY JOE. What's the matter with him?

ESSIE. I think you must remind him of somebody. Let me just try to rustle you up a Coke. (*She starts for the kitchen.*)

BOBBY JOE. If it ain't no trouble.

ESSIE. No trouble at all. (*She exits.*)

DON. (*Shaking his head.*) Lord, *every time* I think I'm cured.

BOBBY JOE. Huh?

BRENDA LEE. (*Changing the subject.*) Well now, how's your sweet mama?

BOBBY JOE. Dead.

BRENDA LEE. Honey, I didn't know!

BOBBY JOE. When I got married, she moved down to Palmetto Sands, Florida an' got herself into the sauce pretty hard, an' one night a while back, she took off all her clothes, 'cept her pantyhose, an' was dancin' on the Interstate at two-thirty a.m. when a sixteen-wheel Bekins movin' van blew her apart at seventy-five miles-an-hour.

BRENDA LEE. That's just horrible!

BOBBY JOE. Well, she always did like to dance.

DON. Is there any chance you just fell from the sky?

BOBBY JOE. No sir, I rode my bike over.

BRENDA LEE. Well, how's your hard workin', adorable daddy?

BOBBY JOE. Dead.

BRENDA LEE. Oh for heaven's sake, never mind! (*She moves away from him.*)

BOBBY JOE. (*Oblivious.*) Felt bad about Mama an' got hisself scarfed up by a threshin' machine.

TOOTH. (*Imitating machine.*) Chomp, chomp! (*Brenda Lee whacks him.*)

BOBBY JOE. I still got one of his shoes.

BRENDA LEE. Yuck! (*Essie enters with a drink.*)

ESSIE. Onliest thing she's got is iced-tea.

BOBBY JOE. It's okeydokey. (*Miz Zifty enters, ready for the parade.*)

MIZ ZIFTY. Here I come. (*Sees Bobby Joe.*) Oh good, they got you a cool drink. You tell Melda she's a heavenly angel.

BOBBY JOE. Yes ma'am.

BRENDA LEE. My zipper jes' won't stay shut.

MIZ ZIFTY. Here, use the safety-pin from my arm. (*Brenda Lee removes it from her.*)

BRENDA LEE. You're a real life saver. (*Doorbell rings.*)

BOBBY JOE. (*Astounded. To Don.*) She got a safety pin in her arm.

DON. (*Deadpan.*) I know. Want one? (*Doorbell again.*)

MIZ ZIFTY. Perhaps this is our mysterious Rhett.

BRENDA LEE. (*Stricken. To Essie.*) Oh my Gawd!

MIZ ZIFTY. (*Suspicious.*) Why don't you let in your guest, Essie? (*Essie, rooted, can only shake her head no.*) Brenda Lee?

BRENDA LEE. Oh my Gawd, oh my Gawd. (*She doesn't move. Doorbell again.*)

BEULAH. (*Entering.*) I'm comin'.

MIZ ZIFTY. (*Stopping her.*) I believe I will see to this visitor myself. (*She goes to the door and opens it. Dr. Kennedy, the black dentist, stands there dressed as Rhett Butler.*)

DR. KENNEDY. Surprise!

MIZ ZIFTY. Jesus wept!

DR. KENNEDY. "Scarlett, never at any crisis of your life have I ever known you to have a handkerchief." (*Miz Zifty tumbles to the ground in a dead faint.*)

BOBBY JOE. Holy Tamoley! (*Brenda Lee begins emitting a high-pitched shriek.*)

BEULAH. (*An order.*) Y'all stop screamin', you dumb twit. (*Brenda Lee does.*)

DR. KENNEDY. Good morning, Miz Scroggins.

ESSIE. Good morning, Dr. Kennedy.

DR. KENNEDY. If you'll excuse me for a minute. (*He kneels by Miz Zifty.*)
TOOTH. (*A low whistle.*) Well now, you're jes' *full* of surprises.
DR. KENNEDY. (*Smiling down at Miz Zifty.*) I see you peeking at me.
MIZ ZIFTY. I am not peekin' at you!
DR. KENNEDY. Out cold, huh?
MIZ ZIFTY. You will leave my house at once.
DR. KENNEDY. We couldn't talk this over?
MIZ ZIFTY. I will scream the house down.
DR. KENNEDY. Well, I'd enjoy that.
MIZ ZIFTY. (*Rising as she carries on.*) Help! Murder!
ESSIE. Miz Zifty . . .
MIZ ZIFTY. Rape! Terrorists! Help! Black Muslins!
DR. KENNEDY. Muslims.
MIZ ZIFTY. What?
DR. KENNEDY. You said, "Muslin." You mean, "Muslim."
MIZ ZIFTY. Are you sure it's not "muslin"?
DR. KENNEDY. "Muslin" is cloth. "Muslims" eat white children.
ESSIE. Harold . . .
MIZ ZIFTY. Help! Help! Out this minute! Bombin' airports, killin' women an' children, highjackin' planes. Where's my pistol?
BEULAH. (*Unmoved.*) In the drawer.
MIZ ZIFTY. Thank you. Sabotagin' everythin'. Outside agitators. Murderin'-liberal-humanist-trash! (*Rummaging for the pistol.*)
BRENDA LEE. Ummmmm, Miz Zifty . . . (*Miz Zifty finds pistol.*)
TOOTH. Hell, look out!
MIZ ZIFTY. GO-rilla!
TOOTH. Look out!
MIZ ZIFTY. (*Fires pistol, which simply clicks.*) What's the matter with this thing?
BEULAH. Ain't loaded.
MIZ ZIFTY. Well, gimme a knife. I'll skin him. I'll sell his hide.
BEULAH. Sure, why not. (*She exits to the kitchen.*)
MIZ ZIFTY. Go back to Africa!

27

DR. KENNEDY. I'm from Detroit.

MIZ ZIFTY. Y'already got the North, overrun the East, ruint our nation's Capitol. Why can't you leave us Brine, Alabama?

DR. KENNEDY. I needed a job, an' you needed a dentist.

MIZ ZIFTY. A white dentist. White like my teeth.

DR. KENNEDY. In that case, I think you're lookin' for an Oriental dentist.

MIZ ZIFTY. A big, tall, blonde, Swedish lookin' dentist outta' Minnesota! (*Beulah re-enters.*)

BEULAH. Here's your knife.

MIZ ZIFTY. That's a cake knife! I can't kill him with a cake knife. Go get me the cleaver.

BEULAH. Sent it out to be sharpened.

MIZ ZIFTY. Well, go next door an borrow one!

BEULAH. Sure, why not. (*She exits.*)

MIZ ZIFTY. For the last time, sir, flee for your life.

DR. KENNEDY. I can't actually.

MIZ ZIFTY. I warn you sir. I have sent for a cleaver.

DR. KENNEDY. I just love "Gone With The Wind." My daddy took us everytime it came out. Funniest damn white people I ever saw.

MIZ ZIFTY. Get out!

DR. KENNEDY. Loved that Clark Gable though. Loved him! Shoulda' seen my imitation. Used to get me laid regular as clockwork.

TOOTH. Mine was Humphrey Bogart. (*He starts stripping off his Ashley Wilkes costume.*)

MIZ ZIFTY. (*To Tooth.*) Animal! (*To Dr. Kennedy.*) Jungle-bunny!

BRENDA LEE. (*Seeing what Tooth is doing.*) Darlin', what are you doin'?

TOOTH. You think I'm goin' into the town square in Brine, Alabama, in front of half the Ku Klux Klan in the state, playin' Ashley Wilkes to his Rhett Butler yer jes' crazier than a whore in a monastery. (*Beulah enters and hands Miz Zifty a meat-tenderizer.*)

BEULAH. Here.

MIZ ZIFTY. This is not a cleaver.

BEULAH. They didn't have one so I brought you a meat-tenderizer.

28

DR. KENNEDY. (*Smiling.*) It is your intention to murder me at high noon with a meat-tenderizer?

BRENDA LEE. (*To Tooth.*) You can't go out there stark nekked.

MIZ ZIFTY. (*To Dr. Kennedy.*) I would not soil my implement. (*She throws it at his feet.*)

TOOTH. (*Still undressing, to Brenda Lee.*) Helluva lot rather be a fool than a target.

ESSIE. (*To Miz Zifty.*) Please don't be angry.

MIZ ZIFTY. Angry? I am far beyond angry.

ESSIE. If you marched with him, you'd be a legend in Brine.

TOOTH. Most likely a real dead legend.

ESSIE. (*To Tooth.*) You white boys are all as yellow as canaries!

TOOTH. Tweet, tweet.

MIZ ZIFTY. And *you* are obviously a deranged person in need of electric-shock therapy.

BOBBY JOE. I ain't yellow.

ESSIE. You are yellow.

BOBBY JOE. I *ain't* yellow.

ESSIE. You *are* yellow.

DON. (*Sitting.*) I *can't* pay the rent. You *must* pay the rent. I *can't* pay the rent. You *must* pay the rent.

ESSIE. (*Pointing to the Ashley clothes Tooth is dropping on the floor.*) Then put those on.

BOBBY JOE. That there Gone-With-The-Window suit?

ESSIE. I *dare* you.

MIZ ZIFTY. I want that Uncle Remus out of here!

ESSIE. If you'd just walk with him, you'd have the biggest crowd your parade ever saw.

MIZ ZIFTY. Scarlett O'Hara would dig turnips out of granite cliffs with her bare bleeding hands before she would be seen, arm-in-arm in public, with a gentleman of color.

DR. KENNEDY. "Gentleman of color" is *nice.*

BOBBY JOE. (*Having mulled over the one challenge no Southern teenager can bear.*) You say you dare me?

ESSIE. Double-dare you. Triple-dare you. Dare you on your dead mama's soul.

BOBBY JOE. Golly!

MIZ ZIFTY. (*To Beulah.*) Get me out of this dress! (*Beulah goes to her, undoes the cinch and begins to help her out of her dress.*)

ESSIE. (*To Bobby Joe.*) Plus, I bet you twenty dollars *and* my ten-speed racin' bike.

BOBBY JOE. The one with the foot stirrups? (*A cry of triumph. A fist raised in the air.*) Hell, I'll do 'er! (*At top speed, he starts putting on the clothes Tooth has taken off.*)

BRENDA LEE. (*To Tooth.*) I thought I threw out that damn undershirt!

DON. (*Watching.*) I think I'm in love.

MIZ ZIFTY. *I* am retiring to my room, having removed this gown as I will officially remove the patronage of the Daughters of the Confederacy from this year's Tara Parade and Ball. And when I return, I assume *you* will return the favor by removing yourself, and your uninvited escort, from these premises.

ESSIE. But he is an educated man! A dentist! He went to Rutgers University!

MIZ ZIFTY. (*Stepping out of the dress in her slip.*) That is, if I may say so my dear young lady, no skin off my butt! (*She exits.*)

BEULAH. My! Ain't that ol' woman got syle? (*She exits after her, carrying the dress.*)

TOOTH. (*To Bobby Joe, who is still dressing.*) You wrong about not being a canary, Horse. They gonna tar you, feather you, an' toss you in the drunk-tank 'til you beg fer birdseed.

BOBBY JOE. Yeah, but she *dared* me.

ESSIE. (*To Dr. Kennedy.*) What in *hell* have I gotten you into?

DR. KENNEDY. This is Brine, Alabama, Mrs. Scroggins. Whatever it is, it beats watchin' the slugs drown in beer. (*Beulah re-enters.*)

ESSIE. What's she doin', Beulah?

BEULAH. Sittin' at her vanity, stark-naked, eatin' peanut brittle and watchin' "The Dukes of Hazard."

TOOTH. (*Now completely undressed, he wears a t-shirt that says "No Sheet" and under that "United Klans of Alabama", and shorts with Playboy nudes printed on them.*) Those boys out there may be small-town, red-neck, dumb-ass, swamp-ramuses, but they ain't crazy. Y'all in here have got hamster-spit for brains, an' when you go out that front door, they gonna skin ya', an' quilt ya'!

DR. KENNEDY. (*To Beulah.*) You wouldn't have a cup of coffee, would you?

BEULAH. A fresh pot with cream from the dairy, an' home-made pralines.

BOBBY JOE. (*Wrestling with his cravat.*) Cain't do these dang watchamacallit, thingmabob, gew-gaw, do-dads.

DON. Here you clumsy thing, let me do that. (*Goes to Bobby Joe.*)

BEULAH. Anybody else want a cup?

BRENDA LEE. I don't believe my shattered system can bear caffeine.

TOOTH. (*At the door.*) Brenda Lee, you comin' with me?

BRENDA LEE. I can't.

TOOTH. You ain't scared?

BRENDA LEE. Scared? Scared?! I am pee-pee petrified! But I can't just leave Essie alone.

TOOTH. You don't know who's out there on that square, spittin' tobacco and waitin' for the parade?

BEULAH. (*Going for the coffee.*) Buncha' toothless, one-eyed, peanut-farmer honkies, who got pork-barbecue for brains. (*She exits.*)

DON. (*Finishing with Bobby Joe.*) Boy, I never saw *anyone* look so tacky, but with your eyes it just doesn't matter.

TOOTH. Jackson "Nut Cutter" Cartwright is out there with his maniac brother Ferd; Ryman Stoner, local National Socialist Nazi; Dim Danny Bone, scalped his wife with a baling knife; an' Big Beaver Wansettler, severed his uncle's arm in a fight with his bare teeth! And hell, those are the moderates.

BOBBY JOE. Guess I'll get in a lot of trouble, huh?

TOOTH. Bobby Joe, trouble don't quite describe it.

BOBBY JOE. Shoot, I'm always gettin' in trouble. Called me "Catastrophe" in high school. Set off a six-car accident. Broke my arm fallin' down one step. Ate a cheeseburger with a bottle-cap in it. Got rabies from my own dog. I guess I'm the right fella for this deal.

DR. KENNEDY. You really man enough to go out there with me, boy?

BOBBY JOE. Shoot, I ain't doin' this for you, mister. I'm doin' this for a ten-speed bike.

DON. My dear young man, I would walk through fire for you. (*He exits to Miz Zifty's room.*)

TOOTH. (*To Dr. Kennedy. Gunshots.*) You gonna do it, huh?

DR. KENNEDY. (*Grinning at Essie.*) I guess so.

TOOTH. (*To Essie.*) You goin' out there with him?

ESSIE. I guess so.

TOOTH. Brenda Lee?

BRENDA LEE. I guess so.

TOOTH. Brenda Lee, I am your devoted husband, but I am too old to die in a remake of "Gone With The Wind." Y'all must be on hard drugs, you know that? Nutcutter Cartwright has got hair on the palms of his hands. Ain't nobody gives a crap about this parade. It's a damn laughin' stock to begin with. Everybody in town thinks that ol' lady belongs in the dribble shop. Hell, the movie hasn't even played here in fifteen years, there's only three of you got costumes on, an' you Woody Woodpeckers is out on parade without the damn character the whole damn book's about anyway! Hell, you don't even have a Scarlett O'Hara!

DON. (*Enters in drag in the Scarlett gown, with hat and lipstick in place.*) "As God is my witness, I will *never* be *hungry* again!"

BOBBY JOE. Howdy-doody-diddley-damn!

BRENDA LEE. Don Savanah, you look just beautiful! (*To Tooth.*) Ain't he wonderful?

TOOTH. It's a walkin' nightmare.

DON. (*Crossing to Tooth as Scarlett.*) "Why Charles Hamilton, you handsome old thing you! I'll bet you came all the way down here from Atlanta just to break my poor heart!"

TOOTH. (*Fleeing.*) Git off me! Stay the hell over there. (*Don makes a feint toward him.*) I swear, I'll burn 'em off an' you'll *be* Scarlett O'Hara!

DON. "Well, you stay right here 'cause I want to eat barbecue with you. And don't go philandering with those other girls, 'cause I'm just as jealous as a Yankee at a Charleston Ball." (*Dropping down to a real "butch" voice.*) Don't worry, Horse, I ain't gonna mess with ya'.

BRENDA LEE. I swear you could be *in* the movie. Hell, you're *better* than the movie.

DON. Well, what do you think, Dr. Kennedy? Want to get out there an' raise a little hell?

DR. KENNEDY. (*Smiling.*) I'm not sure you are exactly what we are trying to say.

DON. Now Dr. Kennedy, we're not prejudiced are we?

DR. KENNEDY. Well, maybe we are . . . just a little.

DON. Isn't life just full of surprises?

DR. KENNEDY. On the other hand, I'm sure you'll admit it's maybe the best idea to tell those boys outside one simple thing at a time.

DON. Yes, I'll admit that's a point. Be a fabulous sequel though
. . . (*Links his arm through Dr. Kennedy's.*) Guess who's coming to
dinner! (*Dr. Kennedy laughs and disengages himself.*)
ESSIE. (*Going over to him.*) I do know one thing . . .
DON. What you know, Aunt Jemima?
ESSIE. (*Kissing him on the cheek.*) You are braver than the "King
Of The Beasts."
DON. Surprised the hell out of me. (*To Bobby Joe.*) Well Ashley,
it's all for you, darlin'? What do you say?
BOBBY JOE. (*Who has been standing, stunned.*) Huh-uh.
DON. Huh-uh?
BOBBY JOE. Huh-uh! No sir. Nosireebob. No way. Huh-uh!
(*Starts taking off the costume.*)
DON. I'd be twice as scared as you.
BOBBY JOE. No sir. Huh-uh.
DON. I dare you.
BOBBY JOE. You dare me? (*Stops for a beat and looks at him.*) No
way, José. Y'all just too rich fer my blood. Meanin' no disre-
spect. (*To Essie.*) Guess I owe you twenty dollars. (*Beulah enters
with the coffee.*)
ESSIE. Never you mind, Bobby Joe.
BEULAH. (*Handing out the coffee.*) Dr. Kennedy?
DR. KENNEDY. Hey, thanks.
BEULAH. (*To Don.*) You care for a cup of coffee, Miss Scarlett?
DON. Just give me the caffeine intravenously.
BEULAH. One lump or two?
DON. (*Helping himself.*) Six. (*Watching as Bobby Joe finishes.*) It's
always been my dream to watch this many men undress in Brine,
Alabama. Unzip me? (*Starting to take off the hat and then the dress.*)
Oh well. There's nothing sadder than a drag queen on the
Fourth of July. (*A loudspeaker outside: "You hear me? One, Two,
Three, One, Two, Three. O.K., listen up now . . . This here is the 23rd
annual Independence Day Tara Parade, an' I wanna hear you boys give
'er a send off." Rebel yells are heard. To Beulah:*) Would you take this
rag out of here, before I cry on it?
BEULAH. (*Taking dress and exiting.*) Oh, the sights I've seen.
TOOTH. You comin' on, Bobby Joe? (*Small marching band
strikes up.*)
BOBBY JOE. Soon as I gits my sneaks on.
BRENDA LEE. (*To Essie, scared.*) Band struck up.
ESSIE. (*Equally scared.*) Don't I know it.

33

BRENDA LEE. (*Sees Don holding the dress he took off.*) You all right, darlin'?

DON. Oh, I may live.

BRENDA LEE. Now jes' don' dwell on it.

DON. Dwell on it?

BRENDA LEE. Jes' forget it, don' think about it.

DON. Jes' not meant to be.

BRENDA LEE. (*An idea.*) Hey you remember, "I'll think of it all tomorrow at Tara. I can stand it then."

DON. (*Picking it up.*) "Tomorrow, I'll think of some way to get him back."

BRENDA LEE. Yes. Yes. (*Both speaking together.*) "After all . . . (*Essie joins the other two.*) . . . tomorrow is another day!" (*They hug and laugh.*)

BOBBY JOE. (*Moving over to Tooth.*) All set.

TOOTH. Brenda Lee Gannet?

BRENDA LEE. Huh-uh. No sir. No way. Huh-uh.

TOOTH. Le's go, Bobby Joe.

ESSIE. Ya'll take care now.

BOBBY JOE. Yes ma'am.

DON. (*To Bobby Joe.*) Better zip up your fly, Horse.

BOBBY JOE. (*Embarrassed.*) Yes ma'am.

TOOTH. So long, Doc.

DR. KENNEDY. (*Putting on the accent.*) See y'all at da' lynchin', Massa Wilkes.

TOOTH. (*Resigned rather than mean.*) Probably ain't too far wrong, Doc. (*Tooth and Bobby Joe exit.*)

DON. Well, at least I know where she keeps the gin. (*Goes to get it.*)

BRENDA LEE. Oh dear.

DR. KENNEDY. (*Energized.*) Tell you what, this is going to be a bonafide hoot!

BRENDA LEE. How can you say that?

DR. KENNEDY. I'm a contrary person, Mrs. Gannet.

ESSIE. (*To Brenda Lee.*) Give me a hand with this snood?

BRENDA LEE. If I can control the shakes. (*Don sits drinking. Brenda Lee goes to Essie. Speaks low.*) You two better be so careful a fly couldn't light on you.

DON. Care for a hit, Reverend?

DR. KENNEDY. (*Rubbing his hands.*) No thanks. Feeling rowdy already.

BRENDA LEE. There, I believe that's it. (*Steps back from Essie.*)

ESSIE. My, the three of us make a pretty poor excuse of a Tara Parade.

BRENDA LEE. Serried ranks, just like the Confederate boys at Gettysburg.

ESSIE. Not even an Ashley Wilkes or a Scarlett O'Hara.

BRENDA LEE. We seem to have run through 'em like a bag of salt-water taffy.

DR. KENNEDY. Mr. Don Savanah?

DON. (*Looking up.*) Say what?

DR. KENNEDY. You care to forfeit your life for the Confederacy as Mr. Ashley Wilkes?

DON. Ashley Wilkes?

BRENDA LEE. That is . . .

ESSIE. What?

BRENDA LEE. . . . it!

DON. I can't do that.

DR. KENNEDY. Yeah you could.

BRENDA LEE. Yes, you can!

DON. But Leslie Howard is such a wimp.

BRENDA LEE. Wimp? He made ten thousand Southern girls jes' throw their skirts right over their heads!

DON. But I'm shakin'!

ESSIE. Please?

DON. Well . . .

BRENDA LEE. We *need* the company!

DON. (*Rising.*) Oh God, why not.

BRENDA LEE. (*Clapping her hands in delight.*) Wake up the snakes, days-a-breaking!

DR. KENNEDY. (*Offering his hand.*) Put 'er there, my man.

ESSIE. (*Laughing.*) Gawd, don't you wish Travis was here?

BRENDA LEE. He'd just beat himself to a pulp.

DON. (*Starting to dress.*) The epitome of Southern manhood. Now this is really drag.

DR. KENNEDY. You know, I don't plan to spend my life in Brine, Alabama, folks. I mean, this has been an interesting gig, but I currently have a wife claiming political asylum in Michigan, and a dead cat nailed to my door. An' after today . . . after today, I might just need to get real serious about selling this practice. So, uh, what I'm trying to say is, anybody who *has* to live here just might want to get off the bus at this stop. See what I mean? (*Nobody answers.*) Don't be shy. (*Nobody answers.*) O.K., Christians. It's an honor to be dinner with you.

BRENDA LEE. I'm so nervous I keep eating my lipstick.

ESSIE. We really do have to scoot.

BRENDA LEE. You better tell Beulah we're on our way.

ESSIE. (*At the foot of the stairs.*) Beulah!

BEULAH. (*Offstage.*) I hear you.

ESSIE. Parade's startin'. You tell Miz Zifty I'll be back bearin' gifts and apologies.

BEULAH. Jes' fainted again.

ESSIE. Miz Zifty did?

BEULAH. Don' worry, I got 'er.

BRENDA LEE. (*At the window.*) Lord, that poor scraggly band's jes' down the block.

ESSIE. Are we really doin' this?

BRENDA LEE. We're really doin' it, darlin'. "Now I lay me down to sleep, I pray the Lord my soul to keep. If I should die before I wake, I pray the Lord my soul to take." There!

ESSIE. O.K., here we go.

BRENDA LEE. Here we go!

BEULAH. (*Appearing dressed as Scarlett O'Hara.*) Y'all ain't goin' nowhere without me, honey!

BRENDA LEE. Jesus-eats-popsicles!

DON. Margaret Mitchell just banged her head on the coffin lid!

BEULAH. (*Turning about.*) How I look?

DR. KENNEDY. I'm not sure, honey, but six Southern states just levitated.

BRENDA LEE. Oh my, oh my, oh my.

ESSIE. Brenda?

BRENDA LEE. (*Grabbing the glass from Don.*) For Gawd's sake, gimme that gin! (*She takes a big swig.*)

BEULAH. If only my momma could see me now.

DR. KENNEDY. Well, I hope she'd have a sense of humor.

ESSIE. (*At the window.*) Here they come!

DR. KENNEDY. (*Gesturing for them.*) O.K. troopers, let's form it up. (*They arrange themselves by the door with Essie and Brenda first, then Don, then Dr. Kennedy and Beulah.*)

BRENDA LEE. I'm as nervous as a long-tailed cat on a porch full of rockin' chairs.

ESSIE. Well, let's just hold hands and squeeze.

DON. I'm doin' it.

DR. KENNEDY. On three.

BRENDA LEE. I just hope there is life after death.

DON. Stick your chests out, girls. We're gonna show those crackers something they have *never* seen before!

ESSIE. (*Crossing herself.*) Jesus and Mary take care of your own.

DR. KENNEDY. One, two, three, hit it! (*They open the door. The band is directly opposite and "Dixie" is being played loudly. Don grabs Brenda Lee's and Essie's hands for a split second.*)

BRENDA LEE. How do I look?

DON. Cute and desperate.

BRENDA LEE. Well, as long as I look cute. Oh my, oh my, oh my.

DON. All right Tara, let's kick ass. (*Essie and Brenda Lee go out, heads high. Don starts to follow, pauses, looks out and then turns back.*) Oh my, oh my, oh my. (*He exits with arms extended like a rock-star greeting his fans.*)

DR. KENNEDY. Dr. Harold Kennedy.

BEULAH. Mrs. Beulah Comstock Ariadne Brown.

DR. KENNEDY. I just have this feeling we aren't going to forget each other.

BEULAH. Those two-bit peckerwoods out there are goin' to choke on a chaw and pee fifteen feet in the air!

DR. KENNEDY. (*Offering his arm, which she takes.*) Frankly my dear, I don't give a damn. (*They exit, leaving the door open, as "Dixie" becomes a crescendo.*)

LIGHTS OUT

37

CLUCKS

BY JANE MARTIN

CLUCKS

The action of the play takes place on the lawn, sidewalk and street fronting the home of Dr. Harold Kennedy in the small Southern town of Brine, Alabama. It is approximately midnight on the Fourth of July. Night sounds. A train passes. Firecrackers in the distance. Travis Scroggins, a powerfully built but worn man of about forty, enters stealthily carrying an airline flight bag. He is dressed in jeans and a plaid shirt with the sleeves rolled up. He hunkers down watching the house for a minute. We can see that the lights are on, though the Venetian blinds are drawn. He looks away towards us, seemingly searching for something. He whistles a bird call. Waits. Trys to find enough light to look at his watch. Whistles again. Nothing.

TRAVIS. Double-eyed-damn! (*Making sure he is unobserved, he takes a sparkler out of his shirt pocket. Searches for and finds a matchbook. There is one left. Looks around once more. He lights the sparkler, throws away the empty matchbook and sings "Bonnie Blue Flag" in something of a stage whisper.*)
"We are a band of brothers,
and native to the soil,
Fighting for the property
We gained by honest toil.
And when our rights are threatened,
The cry rose near and far
Hurrah for the Bonnie Blue Flag
That bears a single star.
Hurrah! Hurrah! For Southern rights, hurrah!
Hurrah for the Bonnie Blue Flag that bears a single star."
(*The sparkler sputters out. He looks quickly around. There is the applause of a single listener from off stage. He hits the dirt. Silence. He whistles. Nothing. He speaks guardedly.*) Yo Ryman? Psssssst? That you, Ryman?
TOOTH. Nope, it's the Avon lady.

TRAVIS. Tooth? What the hell . . .

TOOTH. (*Enters wearing his Shell station coveralls.*) Man, Travis, your bird calls are piss-poor. Sounds like a grackle in the missionary position.

TRAVIS. Sure as hell wasn't whistlin' for you.

TOOTH. Liked your dog-an'-pony show though. Singin' away. You got another sparkler, I'd like to hear "Jesus Wants Me For A Sunbeam." (*Frustrated, Travis growls and hits himself several times on the chest.*) Lord, Travis, don' start in. Thought you wasn't gonna beat yerself up no more.

TRAVIS. You see Ryman?

TOOTH. That boy's crazy as a goggle-eyed perch.

TRAVIS. Never you mind.

TOOTH. Shot off a toe doin' Western fast-draw, an' blew up his own garage messin' 'roun' with explosives.

TRAVIS. You see him or not?

TOOTH. He's down to the station, playin' Pac-Man.

TRAVIS. Crap!

TOOTH. Boys say you got a ride on.

TRAVIS. You blind, deaf, an' dumb, turkey? What you think went on here this afternoon? Hell yes, we got a ride on. You in?

TOOTH. Nosirree, Horse. Hung up m' sheet.

TRAVIS. Yer pussy-whipped, an' Ryman's playin' Pac-Man. Jes' what is it you want, buddy?

TOOTH. Played me some soft ball, dropped by the pie sale, saw me the parade an' took in the fireworks. Thought I'd just come on down here an' see you git shot.

TRAVIS. Saw the parade, huh?

TOOTH. Never saw so many good ol' boys go apeshit at the same time. Colonel Carter got so pissed-off he passed out, an' "Nutcutter" was pickin' his teeth an' damn near bit clean through his index finger.

TRAVIS. Didn't nobody stop 'em though, did they?

TOOTH. Too many Smokies.

TRAVIS. So damn what? Man, it gits me *hot!* You see them coloreds?

TOOTH. Yeah.

TRAVIS. Scarlett O'Hara, Rhett Butler? Paradin' right down the street with our wives! Took six guys t' hol' me down an' a Smokie t' sit on m' face.

40

TOOTH. Yeah, you seemed a little peeved.

TRAVIS. How come you didn't have no clothes on?

TOOTH. Dead drunk. Wasn't marchin' in no African parade.

TRAVIS. Buddy, we better build ourselves an ark 'cause it's the damn end of the world, tha's all I know! Colored in the Tara Parade! Desecratin' the only damn book that's got more literature to it than the damn Bible for Gawd's sake! Miz Zifty's damn maid got up like Scarlett O'Hara fer hell's sake. What the hell kind of South are we livin' in, that's what I want to know? Takin' our jobs, takin' our land, takin' our wives, an now, ding-dang it, they've gone an' takin' our only damn book! Shoot! Essie an' Brenda Lee jes' smilin' an' wavin', big as life an' twice as sassy, sellin' you, me, an' Alabama right down the river, right out in front of Gawd an' damn-all everybody! (*He pounds on his body a couple of times and gives himself a good one to the jaw.*)

TOOTH. Care for an almond?

TRAVIS. You know them almonds is shelled by colored, don't ya'?

TOOTH. Ain't even shelled by humans. Shelled by machine now.

TRAVIS. Well, I don' like machines, and I *sure as hell* don' like colored!

TOOTH. How are ya' on almonds?

TRAVIS. Gotta sit here an' suck m' thumb 'cause Ryman's got the damn sawed-offs.

TOOTH. Yeah, I seen he had yer twelve gauge pump.

TRAVIS. Crazy bastard saws his off too close to the guard-mount. Gonna blow his damn hand off an' hafta play the Pac-Man with his teeth.

TOOTH. You ain't plannin' t' shoot nobody, are ya', Horse?

TRAVIS. Gonna make things hot enough so Rastus over there catches him the next flight outta here back to Sodom an' Gomorrah.

TOOTH. Shoot, his wife left soon as you started nailin' those dead cats to his door. He'll be gone anyway, soon as he can sell the practice.

TRAVIS. What the hell he doin' here, anyroad? Let him pull those chimpanzees' teeth up North.

TOOTH. Hell, it's lucrative, Trav. Ain't a good ol' boy south of Nashville that don't have rotten teeth.

41

TRAVIS. There ain't a coon born good enough to touch a white man's teeth. Hell, I guess I gotta go *git* Ryman.

TOOTH. Tell you what, sport. I wouldn't git within five miles of Mr. Ryman "White Power" Stoner when that crackpot's holdin' a loaded shotgun.

TRAVIS. He'll do what I damn-well tell him, or I'll twist that little make-believe Nazi up till he comes out lookin' like a damn swastika.

TOOTH. Got you a solitaire ride, huh?

TRAVIS. Ain't a white man with two balls left in Brine, Alabama.

TOOTH. Thought y'all still had Billy Q.

TRAVIS. Said he hadda babysit his kids.

TOOTH. Moon?

TRAVIS. Wife wouldn't let him. Dim Danny Bone an' Nutcutter chugged them a gallon of Cherry Bounce, an' somebody jes' propped 'em up against the goal-posts out to the high school. Colonel Carter says his 'lectric wheelchair's broke, an' Mac Bob claims he's got a calf comin'.

TOOTH. Yeah, an' he's most likely its daddy.

TRAVIS. Big damn talkers.

TOOTH. Hell, Horse. Who cares about some Hickville parade where they decorate tricycles with red crepe paper an' pull a pet skunk in a speedo wagon, anyway? Le's you an' me drop by my trailer, eat us a box of vanilla wafers an' kill a fifth a' Rebel Yell.

TRAVIS. I'm on the business of the Invisible Empire here, man.

TOOTH. Don't gimme no Invisible Empire. Hell, that stuff's gotten to jes' be one big ol' panty-raid. Let the air outta a few tires, burn a few crosses, gift-wrap some dog doody an' leave it on the porches. Ol' Beulah caught me hidin' in her zinnias an' called up my mama at the nursin' home an' told on me. That was it for me, buddy! Shoot, Travis, when they shut down the egg picklin' plant, all the coloreds moved to Houston, lef' the rest of us here like flies stuck t' fly paper. Hell, I wish them colored's come back jes' fer company. If we had us a skyscraper, an' we pissed off the top in all four directions, there wouldn't be a thousand people get wet.

TRAVIS. Can't jes' lay down an' play dead.

TOOTH. Can't jes' sheet up an' play Klan.

TRAVIS. You can kick yer manhood in the nuts if y'all want, but I'm standin' up fer America, buddy. I don' want m' boys seein' Red Chinese playin' fer the Dallas Cowboys.

TOOTH. Red Chinese ain't never gonna play fer the Cowboys 'cause they don't use drugs. All that Klan talk about a white-caucasian-righteous-Christian-culture is just pissin' in the wind. Way back when we shoulda' put the coloreds on the boat back t' Africa, nuked them Ruskies down to a low-rise parkin' lot, turned Japan into a miniature umbrella factory, and then seceded an' give them knee-jerk liberals an' Jews the state of New Yawk an' let 'em talk each other to death. But, oh no! Ever' time we got anybody down we jes' let 'em right back up. White man's the victim of moderation, Travis. Hell, we *always* gave a sucker an even break. Thought we done them damn Indians in, an' now they're right back buyin' Maine and drivin' Cadillacs. What to know where we're at Travis? Russians got our know-how, Japs got our money, coloreds got our jobs, Arabs got our women, Jews got our education, liberals got our government, an' all we got left is Dolly Parton and these sad-ass panty-raids . . . an' I ain't too damn sure about Dolly Parton. Hey, Horse, they got us so screwed up you gonna git yourself shot by a stone-Baptist-Nazi while yer tryin' t' make Brine, Alabama safe fer Rhett Butler.

TRAVIS. Well, I'm damn sorry fer a man talks like that on the Fourth of July. Damn sorry.

TOOTH. Listen, buddy. I got this funny feelin' that you take yer one-man Klan to that Nigra dentist's tonight, yer gonna end up showin' yer circumcised to the coroner.

TRAVIS. Looky here, fat man. When the Klavern got down to six, seven members an' y'all wanted me to move up from Klallif to Grand Kludd, I give up Kiwanis an' my Wednesday bowlin' league t' try to git you boys back some pride an' self-respect.

TOOTH. Quit yer bowlin' league, hell. They threw you out the night you ran three straight gutters an' 'en shotput yer ball right through that fifteen thousand dollar pin-setter.

TRAVIS. (*Grinning.*) Now that was a *good* night. (*Tooth laughs. A pause. They stand looking out.*)

TOOTH. This ol' Alabama's a pretty place.

TRAVIS. Yeah, it's a nice place fer poor people.

TOOTH. Hey, I got 'er. Le's see if ol' Eulanie J. wants t' git laid hangin' upside down on the park jungle-gym like she did that one time.

TRAVIS. That was fifteen years ago, Tooth.

TOOTH. Bet she's still practicin'.

TRAVIS. You got some reason you wanta warn me off this ride?

TOOTH. Reason?

TRAVIS. (*Measuring him.*) Reason.

TOOTH. Naw. (*Pause.*) How's Essie?

TRAVIS. 'Bout half crazy. Hell, you seen her paradin' with Rhett Butler.

TOOTH. You was s'posed t' be Rhett Butler.

TRAVIS. (*Hot.*) You gonna walk around with yer wife done up like Lil' Black Sambo?

TOOTH. You piss her off, Horse. Thinks you jes' took on Grand Kludd t' git outta the house.

TRAVIS. How'm I gonna stay in the house with a woman wants me to learn French off a cassette tape? That damn woman don't never let up. Cuts stuff outta the paper an' pastes it on my plate. Finish my grits an' there's "E.R.A." starin' me in the face. Got in some record club. "Couldn't we stay home one night, listen t' Ludwig damn Beethoven?" Shoot! 'At ain't no way fer a man.

TOOTH. Man should be out puttin' cottonmouths in mail-boxes an' shakin' itchin' powder onto people's hung-out clothes by moonlight.

TRAVIS. Them colored's moved out two weeks later.

TOOTH. Moved out 'cause he got him a job off-shore drillin' down t' Texas. Hell, you wanted that job.

TRAVIS. No way, buddy. That foreman was dumb, black an' a Pope-kissin' Catholic.

TOOTH. (*Irritated.*) Hell, yer wife's a Catholic.

TRAVIS. You callin' my wife a Catholic?

TOOTH. She *is* a Catholic.

TRAVIS. (*Furious.*) I know she's a Catholic, but you sure as hell better not call 'er one! Now you callin' her a Catholic or not?

TOOTH. Travis, I been beating you up every Fourth of July since fifth grade, an' the plain fact is I'm wore out with it. Same every time . . . drink us some Buds, drive aroun' litterin', do a little Klanprankin', then you pick a fight an' I ream yer butt up one side an' down the other an' deliver yer bleedin', unconscious body back to Essie. Then she calls the cops on me an' we call it a

44

night. Jes' fer variety, le's go on out t' the auto dump an' I'll sit n' watch while you slam yer head in the car doors.

TRAVIS. I ain't cleanin' yer plow, or goin' t' the auto dump or playin' pineapple upside-down cake with Eulanie J. . . . I got some white man's business to attend to. (*A hooded figure has appeared out of the darkness on the other side of the stage.*)

BOBBY JOE. Y'all freeze! (*Travis hits the dirt with a flying leap. Tooth crouches.*)

TOOTH. Who's that?

BOBBY JOE. Jes' me.

TOOTH. Bobby Joe?

BOBBY JOE. How y'all doin'?

TRAVIS. (*Mortified and furious.*) Goddamnit Bobby Joe! Ow!

BOBBY JOE. Jimminy Cricket, I was jes' kiddin'. (*He is completely robed as a Klansman, marred only by the fact that his robe has been made with a flowered, cotton sheet.*)

TOOTH. (*To Travis.*) Yer nose is bleedin'.

TRAVIS. Prolly broke the damn thing again.

BOBBY JOE. (*Serious. Interested.*) Y'all hit the dirt, huh? That how you did it in Vit Nam?

TRAVIS. Never min' what I did in Vit Nam. I tol' you t' stay offa us.

BOBBY JOE. Wish I'd been in Vit Nam.

TRAVIS. Din't I see you come out of Miz Zifty's house where them Nigras was gittin' up fer the parade?

BOBBY JOE. Jes' spyin' on 'em. Melda sent me on a delivery.

TOOTH. What the hell you got on?

BOBBY JOE. Melda run it up for me on her Singer.

TRAVIS. Love-a-duck, boy! Might as well jump up at a N. double A. C. P. meetin' an' jes' tell those yard apes we be ridin' t'night.

BOBBY JOE. (*Astounded.*) You been to a N. double A. C. P. meetin'?

TRAVIS. Ain't *no* Martin Lucifer coon-show in Brine, Alabama, boy. I'm talkin' about the Klan ridin'.

BOBBY JOE. S'posed t' come on a horse? Where'd you git a horse?

TRAVIS. Din't come on no horse, I come in my Toyota.

BOBBY JOE. You said I oughta jump up at the N.A.A.C.P. an' tell 'em you was ridin'.

TRAVIS. Klan mission's a "ride." Called "a ride." Been that way fer a hundred years.

BOBBY JOE. They ain't had Toyotas fer a hundred years.

TRAVIS. You need a air-controller fer the space between yer ears.

BOBBY JOE. Yer nose is bleedin'.

TRAVIS. Git on home.

BOBBY JOE. Aw, come on Uncle Travis. When I's sixteen y' said I could join up at seventeen, and when I's seventeen y' said eighteen. Well I'm *nineteen* an' I wanna git in on the fun an' make Alabama safe fer white women.

TOOTH. Horny as you are, Bobby Joe, this state ain't never goin' t' be safe fer white women.

TRAVIS. (*Peering.*) What you got on that sheet, boy?

BOBBY JOE. Only one I got.

TRAVIS. You got flowers on that sheet?

BOBBY JOE. Weddin' present.

TRAVIS. (*Astounded.*) You got little bitty violets on yer sheet? You makin' fun on me, Bobby Joe?

BOBBY JOE. Shoot no, Uncle Travis.

TRAVIS. There's a door in yer heart that "funny" don't go through. Place where a man keeps what's sacred. Man don't have a place where there's no laughin' ain't no man, Bobby Joe.

BOBBY JOE. I got a place in my heart.

TRAVIS. There been three American Presidents wore these robes . . .

BOBBY JOE. Harding, Coolidge, an' McKinley . . .

TRAVIS. That's right!

BOBBY JOE. . . . . I 'member 'em 'cause they all sound like air conditionin' companies.

TRAVIS. You got a picture of Jesus in yer house, boy?

BOBBY JOE. Yes, sir.

TRAVIS. What kinda robe he got on?

BOBBY JOE. White robe.

TRAVIS. You damn betcha. Ain't no little bitty violets on that man's robe. (*Takes something out of his pocket.*) You know what this is? (*Holds it out.*)

TOOTH. Lord, don't take that thing out!

BOBBY JOE. It's an eyeball.

TOOTH. Makes me sick to my stomach.

TRAVIS. Glass eyeball. Used to be in Willy Creel's head. Willy had him the Robert E. Lee Diner out to the Trimble Bypass an' he was servin' the colored. Now, I went out there to reason with him. He said he'd serve who he damn-well pleased an' the Klan could go diddle itself on a roto-rooter. Started to walk off an' I hit him so hard with a napkin dispenser his glass eye popped right out.

BOBBY JOE. Popped out?

TRAVIS. (*Makes the sound.*) Pop. Jes' like a champagne cork. Landed in ol' lady Gannet's oatmeal. She's watchin' *us* see, an' next bite she swallows the damn thing whole. When I'd cleaned Willy's plow, I tol' Gannet that eye ever turned up, I wanted it. She's a good ol' girl, said she'd work on it. Few days later, when she delivered my eggs, there was eleven Plymouth browns an' Willy Creel's eye in the egg carton. Had it ever since. Now you take it, to remember a man fights for what's sacred.

BOBBY JOE. Golly, thanks Uncle Travis. Hope I don't throw up.

TOOTH. (*Claps Bobby Joe on back.*) Pretty nice, huh? Y'all come by my trailer, we'll have a drink on 'er. (*A man is heard singing.*)

PRITCHARD. (*Offstage.*)
"Ridin' the night
Come the forces a' light
In the service of bold liberty . . ."

TOOTH. (*Recognizing the sound.*) Pritchard. (*Travis slaps his forehead in dismay.*)

PRITCHARD. (*Enters. Seventy years old. Been drinking. Completely robed, with a Klansman on horseback appliqued on the back. Finishes the song.*)
"Though the tempest may toss
We hold firm to the cross
In the land of the brave and the free."
(*Finishes with a flourish.*) Howdy boys. How*dy* Doody! Wheeee-oooooo! Le's ride!

TRAVIS. You mind keepin' it down to a mild roar, Pritch?

PRITCHARD. S'posed t' sing when y' ride, Sonny.

BOBBY JOE. You got a Toyota too?

PRITCHARD. Dead quiet. Moon, crickets, coon dogs, nothin'

moves . . . then, BANG, we sweep down outta the hills, thunderin' hoofbeats, singin'. Y' look up. There we are, hundreds of us drawn up in a line on the ridge. Silent sentinals.

BOBBY JOE. What ridge?

PRITCHARD. Any ridge.

BOBBY JOE. We ain't got a ridge.

PRITCHARD. On the hill then.

BOBBY JOE. We ain't got a hill.

PRITCHARD. On toppa' the damned Burger King then. What difference does it make?

BOBBY JOE. How you gonna git the horses up on the Burger King?

TRAVIS. Shut the hell up, Bobby Joe! (*Goes to Pritchard.*) Pritch, this here's a pretty serious ride fer a man yer age.

PRITCHARD. Listen here, boy. When I was Gran' Kludd, I usta donate my ol' silks t' yer momma so she could cut 'em up fer diapers for yer extra sensitive butt.

TRAVIS. Gonna fire a cross on the Nigra dentist's lawn, an' they say that boy's got him a gun collection.

BOBBY JOE. Dr. Kennedy? You gonna flame Dr. Kennedy's?

PRITCHARD. What in Peter, John, Paul er Judas you wearin', boy?

BOBBY JOE. Onliest one she had.

PRITCHARD. You cain't go Klannin' around like that.

TRAVIS. Hell, I already tol' him . . .

PRITCHARD. Cain't go ridin' done-up like a giant pair a' whore's panties.

TRAVIS. You git it off *now,* boy.

BOBBY JOE. No disrespect, Uncle Travis, but I jes' cain't do 'er.

TRAVIS. Well, I'm gonna peel ya' like a damn onion an' stuff Melda's sheet up yer butt till yer hair turns red an' y' feel like Raggedy Andy.

BOBBY JOE. Ain't got me nothin' on underneath, Uncle Travis.

TOOTH. You bare-nekked under there?

BOBBY JOE. First time I wore one, an' I din't know. Thought she was maybe like a kilt.

TRAVIS. That's yer Scottish Clan, not yer Ku Klux Klan, ya' damn fool.

PRITCHARD. Man desecrates the Invisible Empire we're s'posed t' give him a tar bath.

TRAVIS. He cain't desecrate it. He ain't in it.

BOBBY JOE. Y'all said I was a trainee.

TRAVIS. A trainee don't go on missions. Trainee don't wear no sacred garb. A trainee jes' buys the beer an' chili-spice Fritos fer the victory celebration.

BOBBY JOE. Hell yes, I got the beer an' the Fritos!

TRAVIS. You git *two* cases a' Bud like I tol' you?

BOBBY JOE. Din't have no Bud . . . . sold out.

TRAVIS. (*Suspicious.*) What kind you git?

BOBBY JOE. Miz Trable said it was a good kind.

TRAVIS. What kind did you *git?*

BOBBY JOE. Lowenbrau.

TRAVIS. (*Completely appalled.*) Lowenbrau!

BOBBY JOE. Light.

TRAVIS. (*Crazed.*) Light?

TOOTH. Easy, big fella.

TRAVIS. Ku Klux Klan can't go 'round suckin' on some dumb-butt, foreign, diet-beer.

PRITCHARD. Cain't even git drunk on 'at stuff, ya' jes' bloat.

BOBBY JOE. I kin go back. They got Miller's.

PRITCHARD and TRAVIS. Miller's?

PRITCHARD. That ain't beer. They make that rat's piss outta ol' fermented oranges.

TRAVIS. Tastes like some kinda cardboard, carbonated . . .

PRITCHARD. Reconstituted, by-God frozen . . .

TRAVIS. Cough-medicine-type, aluminum-tastin' fruit juice!

PRITCHARD. Make ya' toss yer cookies.

TRAVIS. Hey boy, I'm out there lawbreakin' an' killin' an' rapin' an' terrorizin' an' I damn well want me a man's beer! (*A church bell sounds the half-hour.*)

TOOTH. Say compadres, it's 'leven thirty an' the State Cops is gonna be makin' their drunk an' disorderly run, so 'less you're lookin' to do tank time in Hueytown I'd jes' pack this one in.

TRAVIS. Smokies ain't gonna go garbage collectin' till midnight. We'll be here an' gone. Missin' some hands, Pritch. You wanna ride?

PRITCHARD. Does the Pope smoke dope? Hell, yes.

TRAVIS. Tooth?

TOOTH. I jes' cain't help y' out, Horse.

BOBBY JOE. I'll do 'er.

TRAVIS. (*Shaking his head.*) Hell, why not?

PRITCHARD. (*To Bobby Joe.*) Stick yer hand up. Other hand. Now say after me . . . I, Bobby Joe Bigun . . . do before God an' Man . . . most solemnly swear . . . that I dedicate . . . my life . . . my fortune . . . an' my sacred honor . . . to the preservation . . . protection . . . an' advancement of the white race . . . an' to that great order . . . the Knights of the Ku Klux Klan. (*Bobby Joe has answered antiphonally.*) Makes you about half legal.

BOBBY JOE. Golly! Say, we ain't gonna lynch the dentist are we, 'cause I got me two temporaries waitin' on the final fillin's.

TRAVIS. You want some colored puttin' his fingers in yer mouth?

BOBBY JOE. Inside of his hands is white.

TRAVIS. That ain't the point.

BOBBY JOE. Only touches yer teeth with the inside part.

TRAVIS. Bobby Joe . . .

BOBBY JOE. So they ain't technically colored fingers.

TRAVIS. (*Confounded by his stupidity.*) How the hell'd I git into this?

BOBBY JOE. Don' run off Dr. Kennedy, Uncle Travis, I'd have to' git Doc Crasty outta' retirement, an' he got the shakes so bad he drilled me right through the lip.

TRAVIS. You rather have teeth or a white Christian culture, boy? This here's the barn-raisin', Sunday-quiltin', home-made ice cream, lung-guts a' America, an' we sure as hell shouldn't be gittin' our dentists from Africa.

BOBBY JOE. Ain't from Africa, he's from Detroit.

TRAVIS. It's the same damn thing. What the hell he come down here for?

TOOTH. 'Cause he wanted to be a barn-raisin', Sunday-quiltin', home-made ice cream Nigra. Shoot, Travis, ain't no white Christian dentist gonna move down here. We ain't even got a suburb. When Doc Crasty started seein' little green men in yer cavities an' talkin' to yer teeth, an' Mabel made him retire, how long it take us t' git another one? (*Ryman enters unseen. He is dressed in a polyester suit, thin tie and wears small, round, wire-framed glasses.*)

50

RYMAN. Took three years. (*He lays two shotguns down. He also carries his robe in a garbage bag, and an oddly-shaped tool box.*)

TOOTH. Three years!

TRAVIS. (*To Ryman.*) Where the hell you bin'?

RYMAN. I'm here now, ain't I?

TOOTH. So what I'm sayin' is Sambo over there had him some work t' do when he got here 'cause our teeth was fallin' out of our heads. Hell, I had one tooth come out when I bit into a strawberry. Another three years, I'll be gummin' baby food. What say we overlook this one itty bitty measly Nigra on behalf of dental hygiene?

TRAVIS. (*Looking steadily at Tooth.*) There's somethin' wrong with you.

TOOTH. Shoot, we only got three coloreds left . . . Beulah, him an' Beannie. Y'all run them off, yer gonna have ta put yer sheets back on the bed.

PRITCHARD. Y'all lay off Beannie.

RYMAN. (*Working on something in the tool box.*) So's he can fetch yer Hershey bars?

PRITCHARD. Uh-huh, that's right.

RYMAN. Cryin' shame if you ask me . . . ex-associate of the great Colonel William Joseph Simmons, honored founder-honcho of the Ol' Original Klan, pallin' aroun' with the Nigra town drunk.

PRITCHARD. Listen here, boy. I'm the town drunk an' don't you forget it. Things I've seen an' done in this life earned me my drinkin'. I'us drunk yesterday, drunk t'day, an' I'm sure as hell gonna be drunk t'morrow. Now yesterday you was an asshole, an' I'm sure yer jus' as reliable.

RYMAN. Day you go too far, ol' soldier, I'll let you know.

PRITCHARD. Day you let me know, chile, I'll send some friends over t' part yer hair. Now I don't want nobody troublin' Beannie. He's the only one in this God forsaken town knows how t'play two-handed solitaire.

BOBBY JOE. I kin play two-handed solitaire.

PRITCHARD. With yer ding-dong maybe.

TRAVIS. Ain't tryin' to' ruin yer card game, Pritch. Far as I'm concerned, Beannie's a white man in a jigaboo suit. But we let some college-educated Northern Nigra come in here, buy him the best house, drive him a Mercy Benz, shed his wife an' start tippin' his hat t' our women, they gonna flood in here. They gonna work cheap, vote each other in, buy yer grandaddy's land, an' end up sippin' sloe gin on the porch while we're wearin' bandanas, washin' clothes in the creek, munchin' chicken-necks an' dandelion greens, an' hoppin' aroun' singing "Doo-dah, Doo-dah."

RYMAN. (*Extremely animated, a fist in the air.*) Right on, brother, you lay 'em to waste!

TRAVIS. (*Who considers Ryman extremely strange.*) O.K., Ryman.

RYMAN. Mother-humpin' Zionists, the whole bunch of 'em! Commie-faggot-Democratic-pro-busing-fetus-killing-miserable piss-ants.

TRAVIS. You bet, Ryman.

RYMAN. (*Still tinkering with screwdriver and pliers inside the tool box, which contains a bomb.*) White man's down to the last tick of the clock. Last mother tick! All a man's got is time. You don't have time, you don't have nothin' but the rigor mortis. You see this here decade-calendar, stop-sequence, microselective, astro-chronometer, digital-watch? White man designed this. Time's only in the white man's mind. Ain't no colored ever designed a good watch. Why you think they call it "colored people's time"? 'Cause it's late. Why you think there ain't no colored people in Switzerland? 'Cause that's where they make the watches. They lettin' us live fast while they live slow so they can be here when we're gone, brothers! They screwin' aroun' with our life-span. Stealin' the white man's time. Got them a warehouse full of our minutes. An' our only hope . . . the *only* hope is the microprocessor, so we'll know *exactly* where we are down to the milisecond, an' they know it. Them spades made themselves up like Japanese an' snuck in to I.B.M. t' steal that program, an' if the security guard hadn't noticed they was wearin' bright maroon platform shoes, that woulda' been all she wrote, brother! They ain't gonna get our time! Ain't gonna steal our life! I got a surprise for the colored, brothers. You see if I don't. (*He stands for a second. Nobody knows to react. He bends back over his work. A pause.*)

TOOTH. What you doin' there, Ryman?

RYMAN. Jes' puttin' the mustard on a dynamite sandwich.

BOBBY JOE. You kiddin' me?

PRITCHARD. (*To Bobby Joe.*) Git on back, boy.

RYMAN. Gonna be the space program's first Nigranaut. Put the coon on the moon.

TOOTH. But that ain't *really* dynamite, right?

RYMAN. Read about that asphalt company in Birmingham got their 'splosive shed robbed? Hey, was that my day in Birmingham er not?

TOOTH. This here's a cross burnin', Ryman, not a nuclear attack.

RYMAN. That coon called me crazy.

TOOTH. Only after you peed on his car.

RYMAN. Think he's so high an' mighty? Well, there's gonna be tarbaby in the treetops tonight. (*Returns his concentration to the bomb.*)

TRAVIS. (*Tooth and he exchange looks. Travis walks over to Ryman.*) How'd the Pac-Man go, Ryman?

RYMAN. Got me three hundred thousand.

TRAVIS. On one quarter?

RYMAN. Din't finish the game 'cause I knew y'all was waitin'.

TRAVIS. Man that good oughta git his quarter back.

RYMAN. Machine don't never give you yer quarter back.

TRAVIS. (*Tossing a quarter on the ground.*) Well tha's the difference 'tween a man an' a machine, ain't it? Go on, pick it up.

RYMAN. Pick it up yourself, cowboy.

PRITCHARD. Y' really oughta pick that one up, Ryman. It's a silver one 'thout any copper.

TOOTH. (*Smiling.*) You scared t' pick it up, Ryman? (*Ryman bends over to pick it up and Travis kicks him in the butt and sends him sprawling.*)

TRAVIS. When it's time for the dynamite, Ryman, I 'magine you'll hear about it from the Grand Kludd.

RYMAN. (*Rising and brushing himself off.*) I got that down in my book.

PRITCHARD. Mus' be a reg'lar historical novel by now.

BOBBY JOE. (*Serious and concerned. He picks up the quarter.*) Here, y' forgot yer quarter. (*Ryman takes it.*) Want me t' pick up yer gold-plated pen?

TRAVIS. (*Ryman picks up his pen and puts it away.*) Got the cross in yer pickup, Ryman? (*Ryman nods yes.*) 'Leven footer? (*Ryman nods yes.*) Well, go git it man. It ain't gonna walk over here by itself! (*Ryman goes. Travis turns to Bobby Joe.*) Go on boy, make yerself useful. (*Bobby Joe starts to go, then turns back.*)

BOBBY JOE. I'm in the Klan. In the Invisible Empire.

TOOTH. Yeah. You're some tough hombre now.

BOBBY JOE. Golly! (*He exits.*)

TOOTH. That Ryman's so mean he must spit formaldehyde.

PRITCHARD. When he was a boy, he'd sneak around the neighborhood at suppertime and stick them jalapeño peppers in ever'body's dog-dishes. Them hounds took off straight-up like helicopters. (*Indicates the dynamite sticks.*) What we gonna do with them firecrackers, Trav?

TRAVIS. (*Moving them to one side.*) I'll jes' take 'em on home with me.

TOOTH. Sure. A man cain't never have enough dynamite.

BOBBY JOE. (*Offstage.*) Yo, Tooth. Give us a hand, will ya'?

TOOTH. (*To Travis.*) You jes' cain't read between the lines, can ya'?

TRAVIS. You gonna babysit me, you might's well give the man a hand.

TOOTH. (*Calling to Bobby Joe.*) I'm comin'. (*Starts off.*) You know how many Klansmen it takes t' unload a cross?

PRITCHARD. How many?

TOOTH. Jes' two, but then you got t' rub 'em together t' start the fire.

TRAVIS. (*Pritchard laughs. Tooth exits.*) Hey, you think we're dumb?

PRITCHARD. You mean can we tell a hawk from a handsaw?

TRAVIS. (*Hits himself.*) I mean I mus' be a damn Mongoloid moron if I'm in the same damn world with Ryman Stoner.

PRITCHARD. Ol' Ryman, he's purt' near smart, so I'd say we're better off dumb. Shotguns, dynamite, pipe bombs, chemicals. Like a bunch a' two-bit A-rab go-rillas. Ol' days all we had was a rope.

TRAVIS. Ever seen you a lynchin', Pritch?

PRITCHARD. One. Wahalak, Mississippi in twenty-two. Tossed my cookies for three days. When that neck snaps, it's louder 'an a twenty-two calibre. Blood spurt fifteen feet out the nose. After he's dead, he'll twitch two hours. Oh, I wasn't in on it . . . musta' been 'bout twelve. My daddy held me up so's I could see. There was four men fainted an' one man threw his hat in the air. Tried t' sing "Onward Christian Soldiers", but din't nobody know all the words. Daddy asked me did I want the man's shoelaces fer a souvenir . . . but I didn't want 'em. Yeah. I only seen one lynchin'.

TRAVIS. How long you been Klannin'?

PRITCHARD. 'Smite over fifty years.

TRAVIS. That long, huh? How come we ain't never won the sum'bitch?

PRITCHARD. Cain't say.

TRAVIS. (*Putting on his robes.*) Well, it's sumpin' to do. Wears me out though.

PRITCHARD. Saw Essie in the Parade. (*Travis hits himself.*) Heard she slep' over to Lurlene's two, three days last week. (*Travis hits himself.*) Trouble in the bed, or in the head?

TRAVIS. Says she's read me twice an' she knows how I come out.

PRITCHARD. Yeah, I had three wives an' they were all hell for variety.

TRAVIS. When it goes bad, can ya' git it back?

PRITCHARD. Well, I couldn't. Course I'm dumber than a banana pizza so it don't signify. My first wife was in the female Klan.

TRAVIS. No kiddin'?

PRITCHARD. Sure. Called it the S.A.C.: Sambo Amusement Company. She was the Queen Cyclops of the Yazoo City Chickadee Klavern. First all female Kalvern an' marchin' band in the state. All'us carried honey an' sand in her purse t' pour in the colored's gas tanks. We were there in Carolina in thirty-six when they burned them a hunnert an' sixteen foot cross. Set the record. Later on, we'd work the truck stops t'gether, order some coffee, read the paper, then she'd slap it down an' holler out, "Gawdamighty honey, the Nigras is takin' over everythin'." Some truck jockey cross the room'd say "Amen", an' we'd git him fer a ten dollar donation. Nice when the husban' an' wife has the same hobby.

TRAVIS. How'd you lose her?

PRITCHARD. Run off with an Imperial Wizard at a Klan Bake. Heard she died of pneumonia runnin' the bottle toss booth at the Fargo, North Dakota State Fair.

TRAVIS. Essie don't like the Klan.

PRITCHARD. Lotta' the women don't.

TRAVIS. She says one night some Nigra's gonna send me home in a jello mold.

PRITCHARD. (*Indicating dentist's house.*) They say this one's got him more guns than the Muslins.

TRAVIS. Yeah, he's a real humdinger. (*Ryman, Tooth and Bobby Joe enter carrying the cross. It is at least ten feet long.*)

BOBBY JOE. Hold 'er, hold 'er, gotta change my grip.

RYMAN. Lay it here, anyroad. It ain't doused.

TOOTH. (*Putting it down.*) Breakin' my damn back.

RYMAN. (*Heads out.*) I'll git the kerosene.

BOBBY JOE. (*To Travis and Pritchard.*) You know what's in his truck? Four rifles, a pistol, eight wooden clubs, a blackjack, brass-knuckles and a hypodermic syringe!

TOOTH. Prob'ly the only way he kin git a goodnight kiss.

BOBBY JOE. (*Holding up joint.*) This was on the dash. You think it's Mary-juana?

TRAVIS. Hell, bein' it's Ryman, he prob'ly smokes used kitty-litter. (*Ryman re-enters, now in his robe.*)

RYMAN. Any you boys got some kerosene?

TRAVIS. Got what?

PRITCHARD. You mean you ain't got any?

RYMAN. Musta' drove off without her.

TOOTH. You got any kerosene, Trav?

TRAVIS. (*Shakes his head no.*) Pritch?

PRITCHARD. I had any I'd drink it.

TRAVIS. Well, damn it t' hell . . .

TOOTH. Ryman, if the las' woman on earth was waitin' on you t' come by an' procreate up another human race, you'd forget t' bring yer pecker.

RYMAN. You name's goin' in my book, bigmouth.

BOBBY JOE. Got me a Bic lighter. We could break 'er open an' git that fluid on there.

TOOTH. Yer a thinkin' man's thinkin' man, Sunny Jim. (*Bobby Joe starts to hand the lighter to Tooth, but Ryman reaches in.*) Hey!

RYMAN. S'my cross.

TRAVIS. Dang it Ryman . . .

RYMAN. S'my cross! (*Pulls at the lighter, trying to get it open.*)

TOOTH. You gonna break it open, or jes' jerk it off?

RYMAN. Hard t' git a grip.

56

TOOTH. (*Gestures for it.*) Here.

RYMAN. Jes' hold yer water.

BOBBY JOE. Let me do 'er. (*There is a lot of light pushing and jockeying for position.*)

TOOTH. Git offa' me.

RYMAN. Git offa' *me.*

BOBBY JOE. Melda says I got hands like a' ape.

RYMAN. Piss-ant li'l thing.

TOOTH. Gimme the damn thing! (*Takes it.*)

PRITCHARD. Hey Tooth . . .

TOOTH. Lemme be.

PRITCHARD. Oughta snap the top off.

TOOTH. (*Working with his teeth.*) Huh?

PRITCHARD. Snap 'er.

TOOTH. Hell, I cracked a tooth.

BOBBY JOE. Says t' *snap* it.

TOOTH. Well shoot.

PRITCHARD. You hear me?

TOOTH. Say what?

PRITCHARD, BOBBY and TRAVIS. Snap it!!

TOOTH. (*Just as loudly.*) Dammit, I cracked a tooth!!

TRAVIS. Shhhhhhhhhhh!

PRITCHARD. Here, try m' buck knife.

TOOTH. I said cracked it, not *extract* it.

PRITCHARD. I mean use it on the . . .

BOBBY JOE. (*Overexcited.*) I got it. I got it! (*Grabs lighter.*)

TOOTH. Hey . . .

TRAVIS. Hol' on . . . (*Bobby Joe throws it down.*)

TOOTH. No, Bobby Joe! (*He stomps it. It breaks and liquid runs out.*)

PRITCHARD. He got 'er!

BOBBY JOE. (*Topping him.*) I got 'er!

PRITCHARD. (*Slapping him on back.*) Yesiree!

BOBBY JOE. We're gonna ride! (*Travis, Tooth and Ryman stare mournfully at him. He sees them. Looks at the ground. Gets the point.*) Oh-oh.

TOOTH. You bake all the brains in Alabama in a pie, you'd still have room fer all twenty-four blackbirds.

RYMAN. (*Pulls out another Bic.*) I got one. (*Pulls a pistol out of the shoulder holster and aims at top of the Bic.*)

TRAVIS. No! (*Pulls it out of Ryman's hand.*) Way you shoot, Ryman, we'll be up all night lookin' fer yer damn finger, plus you'll have the whole town all over us. (*Travis snaps the Bic neatly in half.*) There. (*Starts the cross. Ryman intercepts him.*)
RYMAN. It's my lighter. (*Takes it over and sprinkles fluid on the cross.*) Y'all gimme a hand here. (*Bobby Joe, Travis and Tooth go over to help.*) You down there. All right, le's do 'er. (*They lift the cross.*)
TRAVIS. Foot it.
BOBBY JOE. O.K., now.
TOOTH. Comin' on.
RYMAN. Easy.
TRAVIS. We got 'er. We got 'er. She straight, Pritch?
PRITCHARD. Little left.
TOOTH. O.K. now?
PRITCHARD. Little right.
TRAVIS. That it?
PRITCHARD. Little left.
TOOTH. (*Leaving the cross. Walks over to look with Pritchard.*) Good gravy, man, which way you want 'er?
RYMAN. Hey, this here's heavy y'know?
PRITCHARD. Tol' ya', more left.
TOOTH. Lef', hell. Look at the pine tree. More right!
PRITCHARD. An' I tell ya' more left!
TRAVIS. (*Leaving the cross and coming to them.*) Gotta do ever' damn thing m'self. (*The cross is now too heavy for the two remaining men.*)
RYMAN. Hey.
BOBBY JOE. Hey.
RYMAN. Hey!
BOBBY JOE. Look out! (*The cross crashes to the ground.*)
TOOTH. (*A brief pause.*) Well, O.K., so tha's done.
PRITCHARD. Tol' ya' more left.
RYMAN. (*Starting for Pritchard.*) You senile ol' idiot.
TRAVIS. Jes' cool *off.* Look, we'll jes' light 'er up lyin' on the ground.
TOOTH. What's the manual say on that, Pritch?
PRITCHARD. Manual says if y'd gone more left y' wouldn't have t' ask what the manual says.

TRAVIS. 'Member, we done 'er lyin' down at the Library, lef' a real good scorch mark.

RYMAN. (*Frustrated.*) Hell, whatever. (*All except Pritchard start for the cross.*)

PRITCHARD. Need a vote. (*Travis turns back.*)

TRAVIS. What's that?

PRITCHARD. Manual says we need a vote.

RYMAN. Ain't got the time, y' ol' fool.

PRITCHARD. (*Implacable.*) Says in the sacred code.

RYMAN. Yer damn rulebook's the only thing in Alabama more decrepit than you are.

PRITCHARD. Whyn't you use a grenade fer a suppository?

TRAVIS. Awright, awright! All present wants t' light 'er up lyin' down, raise yer hands? (*All but Pritchard do so.*)

RYMAN. Let's do 'er! (*They all head for cross, except Pritchard.*)

PRITCHARD. S'posed to be a secret ballot.

TOOTH. (*To Travis.*) An' when we get through it says we gotta drink Lowenbrau beer.

TRAVIS. Ryman, gimme that hand-gun.

RYMAN. What for?

TRAVIS. So you can be alive fer another two minutes. (*Ryman hands it to him.*) Pritch, I'm forty years old, been laid off six months, my wife's turned colored on me, m' oldest boy ran over m' neighbor's blue-ribbon Pekinese on his motorbike, I can only git it up oncet a week an' I'm goin' t' light that cross lyin' down. Now if that ain't in yer goddamn manual jes' go ahead an' shoot me. (*Gives pistol to Pritchard and goes to the cross. Searches in pocket for matches, finds nothing.*) Somebody give me a light. (*A pause. They look at each other.*) Gimme a match. (*They look in their pockets.*) Gimme a lighter! (*They look at him.*) Gimme two goddamn sticks! (*Bobby Joe does. Travis breaks them and throws them at him.*) Colored, hell. We oughta run *ourselves* outta' Alabama. (*Sound of an approaching car.*)

RYMAN. Car comin'.

TOOTH. Where? (*Flashing police beacon hits them from off.*)

BOBBY JOE. State Cops.

PRITCHARD. What'll I do with this gun?

RYMAN. Shoot fer the tires.

PRITCHARD. I ain't shootin' at the State Cops.

TOOTH. Stick it in yer belt.

RYMAN. Dynamite. Where's the dynamite?

TRAVIS. Ryman . . . Hey, jes' look casual.

ZITS. (*From offstage.*) How's it hangin'?

BOBBY JOE. Hey, aren't you . . . ?

ZITS. (*Twenty-two years old. Pock-marked face. High nasal voice. A recent graduate of the police academy.*) Y'all havin' you a bang-up Fourth?

BOBBY JOE. Z'at you, Zits?

ZITS. Dang it!

TOOTH. Zits?

ZITS. Aw, don' call me that. I got me a new face cream. Workin' real nice.

BOBBY JOE. (*A high school cheer.*)
We got the doughnut
You got the hole
(*Zits joins him.*)
Les' go Rebels
Roll, Roll, Roll!

ZITS. You Bobby Joe Bigun, ain't ya?

BOBBY JOE. Hell, yes! Hey, I was a freshman when you was a senior! Hey, y'all remember Zits dontcha? Had the lowest completion record of any quarterback in the history of Brine High.

TRAVIS. Good goin'.

ZITS. Well, I was playin' hurt.

BOBBY JOE. Got sacked fourteen times in one quarter.

TOOTH. Oh, yeah?

ZITS. I'm a State Policeman now though.

TOOTH. That's a real scary thought.

ZITS. Evenin' Mr. Pritchard. Evenin' Mr. Scroggins. How you doin', Tooth?

BOBBY JOE. This here's Ryman B. Stoner, born in Brine but jes' moved back . . . sells them Apple computers.

ZITS. Hey, you ain't the Ryman Stoner put that seven-hundred-thousand on the Pac-Man at the Kinkler-Tutweiler Hotel over t' Hueytown, were ya'?

RYMAN. Seven hunnert an' thirty.

ZITS. Gawdamn! Gawd Damn! Yer jes' a Lord-lovin' legend in yer own time! We retired that damn machine with a sixteen pound sledge, in yer honor. You got the hands of a damn safe-cracker! You mind authographin' my undershirt.

RYMAN. Well . . .

ZITS. Gotta magic marker?

RYMAN. Well, sure.

ZITS. (*Tearing open his shirt, hands Ryman the marker. Talks while Ryman writes.*) Man, oh man, wait'll the boys see this! Jes' write "Happy Packin' to my ol' buddy Zits." Shoot, I'm a *player.* Won't even answer a burglary call if I got a good screen goin'.

RYMAN. (*Finishing.*) There ya' go.

ZITS. Fubbin'-fantasterrific, man! Lemme shake the king's joystick.

RYMAN. Say what?

ZITS. The hand that done seven-hundred-mother-thousand. (*Shakes Ryman's hand.*) Say Mr. Scroggins, that your Toyota back over there?

TRAVIS. Might be.

ZITS. Right on! See Mr. Scroggins, I'm pleased t' tell you, I'm givin' you my first ticket. First citation as a State *Po*liceman. See, this here's my first night on m' own. Fubbin' blast, man! You know what's funny? I got t' shoot me somebody last week, but I jes' ain't been privileged yet t' hand out a traffic violation. Seems like it should might go t' other way around. You know, give out a ticket first an' then shoot somebody. Well, life's funny, ain't it?

TOOTH. I'd say life was funny, wouldn't you Trav?

TRAVIS. (*To Zits.*) You got a match?

ZITS. Hey, I don' smoke man, that stuff kills ya'. You know, it's funny first time y' shoot somebody. Goes down real easy. (*Pulls out pistol.*) Truth is, I didn't even mean t' shoot this guy. It was real funny, see, they tol' me t' fire a warnin' shot so I aimed high, but I had the damn hiccups. Drilled that ol' boy clean. Bang. (*The gun fires accidentally. Zits slaps it.*) Dumb ol' thang. M' partner said don't take it t' heart 'cause he was most likely a bur-glar . . . or somethin'. Hey, you know what? Dead people look real dead. I mean it surprised me, you know, how dead they look. (*Puts gun in his holster. They all sigh in relief.*)

TRAVIS. What you givin' me a ticket for?

ZITS. Mr. Scroggins, I'm jes' pleased as punch t' tell you your Toyota is one hunnert percent illegal parked in a handicapped zone. Ain't that great? Purty good luck fer me. See, they tol' me I better git out there tonight an' jes' arrest the hell outta' somebody's butt.

TRAVIS. You gonna arrest me at midnight on the Fourth of July fer parkin' in a handicapped zone?

ZITS. Them crips got a hard life, Mr. Scroggins. You didn't have any arms er legs you'd want a good place t' park. Now I called 'er in t' git ya' towed off, but you got t' go anywhere I'd be right pleased t' ride ya'. Show y'all the gadgets in m' cruiser. (*Focusing on Bobby Joe's outfit.*) Say . . . what y'all up to out here?

TOOTH. Uhhh . . .

BOBBY JOE. Up to?

PRITCHARD. Uhhh . . .

TRAVIS. Well, we uh . . .

TOOTH. Jes', you know . . .

BOBBY JOE. Jes', you know . . .

PRITCHARD. Screwin' around.

TRAVIS. Yeah.

BOBBY JOE. Right!

TRAVIS. Jes' screwin' around.

ZITS. (*Noticing the cross.*) An' whatcha doin' with this here thing?

PRITCHARD. Lef' over from the Revival. Brother Thunder's travelin' tent savin'. You 'member that, dontcha Ryman?

RYMAN. Oh sure . . . sure.

TOOTH. Yeah, Brother Thunder. I got saved couple a' times that night. Had t' go out t' pee in the middle. Come back in, bang, they saved me again.

ZITS. This here's a ride, ain't she?

TOOTH. A ride?

PRITCHARD. Wha's a ride?

ZITS. Little Klan bang. Little sheet treat.

PRITCHARD. Now looky here, Zits . . .

TRAVIS. (*Cutting across him.*) Yeah, that's right. The Klan. We gonna leave us a little callin' card on a Nigra's lawn, boy. Now jes' what you gonna do about it?

ZITS. (*A dramatic standoff.*) A ride, huh? (*He and Travis stare at each other.*) Hot damn! Got my robes in the car! (*He races off to the cruiser.*)

PRITCHARD. That boy got him zits on the brain.

RYMAN. He's all right.

TOOTH. You jes' like him 'cause he shook yer joystick.

TRAVIS. What Klan you figger that boy's in?

RYMAN. Ain't the Ol' Original, 'cause I'd know it. Could be the Dixie Knights or the Reconstituted. Read where they was workin' this part of the state.

TOOTH. Din't you have yer own Klan oncet, Pritch?

PRITCHARD. Called us the Emerald Rebs. Had us black hoods an' green satin bowlin' jackets. Tried t' git us some busin' started.

BOBBY JOE. Git it started?

PRITCHARD. All the Klans was hell on busin', but we din't have us none down here, so we figgered we git us some started so we could stop it. Coloreds din't want it though, an' it was kindy embarrassin'. They'd picket us. Finally there wasn't enough Emerald Rebs fer a hand a' stud poker, an' we quit.

TRAVIS. Trouble with this damn country is everybody stays home 'steada' participatin'. (*Zits returns, carrying his robes and a big bowl of popcorn.*)

ZITS. Ready to ride! Any a' you gents want you some popcorn?

BOBBY JOE. Where's you git it this time of night?

ZITS. Got me a battery-operated popper in the cruiser, plus I got me a Sony T.V. an' some marital aids, case I run inta somethin' good. (*Claps his hands.*) Man, I cain't wait till we git that fubbin' cross goin'!

BOBBY JOE. Ain't got a match.

ZITS. No fire huh? You jes' watch me. (*Heads up to Dr. Kennedy's front door.*)

TRAVIS. Where the hell you goin'?

ZITS. Little Klangenuity. (*Rings door bell.*)

TRAVIS. (*To the others.*) Git back! (*They take cover.*)

ZITS. Hey, y'all scaredycats. (*Dr. Kennedy opens the door. He wears a summer-weight sport coat and slacks.*)

DR. KENNEDY. Yes?

ZITS. Officer Puckett, sir. State Highway Patrol. Sorry to disturb you, sir, but I saw some men of a suspicious nature near yer property, an' I found this . . . (*Shows Dr. Kennedy the robe over his arm.*) . . . on yer lawn.

DR. KENNEDY. Uh-huh. Very kind of you to be concerned.

ZITS. Yes sir. Well, I just wanted to let you know. And to assure you that we'll keep an eye open.

DR. KENNEDY. Well, I'd appreciate it Officer Puckett. The good ol' boys we have here tend to remember I was a Special Forces night weaponry expert in 'Nam, so they run through my flower beds every once in a while, but they're basically committed to stayin' live bigots instead of dead slipcovers.

ZITS. 'Nam, huh?

DR. KENNEDY. Right. 'Nam. Well, goodnight to you then.

ZITS. Say, uh, excuse me, but see, I got the cigs but no twigs, if you know what I mean. Need me a light t' git through the night.

DR. KENNEDY. Just what is it you want, Officer?

ZITS. Oh, jes' a match, mainly.

DR. KENNEDY. (*Reaches in his pocket.*) Take the pack.

ZITS. Purely appreciate it. (*Turns to go.*)

DR. KENNEDY. Officer? Is your first name Emory, by any chance?

ZITS. Hey. Yes sir. How'd you know that?

DR. KENNEDY. Well, for one thing, your name tag's sticking out of your robe. (*He closes the door on the astounded Zits.*)

TRAVIS. Fooled him right down to the ground.

PRITCHARD. Your momma oughta sew a name tag on your pee-pee, so the toilet bowl'd know who you were.

ZITS. Got the matches, din't I?

RYMAN. Look, I got me a barn t' burn down, so I'd like t' git goin' here.

TRAVIS. Le's do 'er.

PRITCHARD. This a first warnin' or a second warnin'?

TRAVIS. Already nailed a cat to his door.

PRITCHARD. S'posed t' cut off a coon head an' stick it on the door handle.

TRAVIS. Damn it Pritch, it's late. I ain't chasin' no racoons.

PRITCHARD. (*Adamant.*) Gotta leave somethin' disgustin' on his front step.

BOBBY JOE. Got me some melted M & M's in my pocket.

TRAVIS. (*Irritated.*) That's jes' fine! Light 'er up, Ryman.

PRITCHARD. S'posed t' sing "Ol' Rugged Cross."

TRAVIS. (*Crazed.*) For Gawd's sake, sing it! (*Pritchard starts.
They join in. At the end, Ryman leans down with the matches.*)
RYMAN. Well, turkey-turds-in-a-bowl-a-grits!
TRAVIS. (*In a quiet fury.*) Now what?
RYMAN. These ain't matches, they're rubbers. Prophylactics!
TRAVIS. They are *what?*
RYMAN. "Royal Sultan super sensitive. Money back guaran-
tee." (*Tooth falls down laughing.*) This ain't funny! (*Travis starts to
laugh.*)
PRITCHARD. He jes' wanted ya' t' have a good time, Ryman.
(*The laughter is now general, with the exception of Ryman.*)
TOOTH. (*Looking at the pack.*) "Extra small." Hell, Ryman, he
knew they was for you! (*They all roar with laughter.*)
RYMAN. This ain't funny. (*Gales of laughter.*) Y'all ain't s'posed
t' laugh at a white man.
TOOTH. Put 'em on yer joystick. (*They fall about.*) This way
yer sheep won't git pregnant.
RYMAN. (*Yelling at the house. Pounding on the door.*) Who you
think you are? Who you think you are, Nigra? You think yer
King Coon, dontcha? You're screwin' with the white man,
monkey-breath. (*Moves center in front of the door.*)
"Black may be beautiful,
An' tan may be grand,
But white's still the color
Of the Big Boss Man."
(*The door is opened and Dr. Kennedy hits Ryman full in the face with a
bucket of water.*) Son-of-a-bitch. (*Ryman races across the stage to
where the shotguns have been left.*)
TOOTH. (*The following dialogue overlaps right up to the shot.*) Hey,
hol' on, Ryman.
TRAVIS. Git him.
TOOTH. Hey.
TRAVIS. Git him!
BOBBY JOE. Git that twelve gauge. (*Zits grabs Ryman but is
shaken off.*)
PRITCHARD. Plain crazy.
TOOTH. Watch it.
TRAVIS. Come on Ryman . . .
RYMAN. Lemme go.

TOOTH. Grab a holt a' that mother . . .

RYMAN. Lemme go.

PRITCHARD. Loaded. Look out!

TOOTH. Git it.

PRITCHARD. Git it. (*Ryman breaks free.*)

TOOTH. Je-sus!

BOBBY JOE. Hit the dirt.

TRAVIS. Rymannnnnnnnnnn! (*Ryman fires at the house, breaking the window. A woman's scream is heard.*)

PRITCHARD. Somebody in there. (*Ryman levels the shotgun again. Travis tackles him.*)

TRAVIS. You damn lunatic. (*Dr. Kennedy appears at the door carrying an automatic weapon.*)

ZITS. Y'all git down!! (*Dr. Kennedy lets go with a burst of automatic fire, raking the stage. The Klansmen flatten, faces in dirt. A moment. No one is hit.*)

DR. KENNEDY. All right, spooks. On your feet. Move it. (*They begin to rise.*) Hands on your head. Both hands. Kick that shotgun out of there. (*Travis does.*) Move in where I can see you. Move! Now, a little light on the subject. (*Flips an outside switch. The yard floodlights come on.*) Now, who we got here. (*To Tooth, the only one without a robe.*) Well, as I live an' breathe, it's Ashley Wilkes. All right, let's have a look. Get 'em off. (*No one moves.*) I said get 'em off. (*He fires a shot in the air. The men rip off their robes in a rush. Bobby Joe is, of course, nude. Dr. Kennedy looks at him.*) For God's sake, put 'em back on! (*They do.*) There is nothing more depressing than a naked white man. Hands on heads! Move it. Say, weren't you boys singin' "Ol' Rugged Cross"? My momma used to sing that to me. I always did enjoy music. You got any other selections? A few tunes. "Sawnnee River"? "Ol' Black Joe"? No? Shoot. I'm a fool for harmony. Hey, you remember, "I'm A Little Teapot", from second grade? Yeah, you do. "I'm a little teapot, short and stout. This is my handle. This is my spout."

BOBBY JOE. Shoot, I know that one.

DR. KENNEDY. Sure you do! Let's give it a try. (*He leads them in song. Travis abstains.*)

ALL.

"I'm a little teapot,

66

Short and stout.
This is my handle,
this is my spout.
When I get all steamed up,
Hear me shout.
Tip me over and pour me out."
(*Travis stands fixated on Dr. Kennedy.*)
DR. KENNEDY. Hey, there is just no doubt about it. You guys have got natural rhythm. One more time . . . (*Fires shot. They sing. He encourages them.*) Louder! (*They finish the second time.*) Very good. Now, with gestures! Move! (*He fires a shot. All dance but Travis.*) Yes, sir! Motown sound! Uh-huh! Now spin. Go on, spin! (*Fires shots in the air as they spin. A woman appears in the doorway. It is Essie, Travis' wife.*) That's real good . . . now . . .
ESSIE. You 'bout through funnin' with 'em, Harold?
DR. KENNEDY. Yeah. Just about. (*The Klansmen stop. They stare at Essie, dumbfounded. Tooth lets out an involuntary whistle and shakes his head.*)
ESSIE. Who you whistlin' at, Tooth Gannet?
TOOTH. (*Touches Travis' shoulder.*) Tried to tell you, Buddy. (*Travis doesn't react.*)
DR. KENNEDY. Now boys, it's the Fourth of July, an' we all had us a real good time and I don't mind fooling with you as long as everybody's *sure* it's fooling.
TRAVIS. What the hell you doin', Essie?
DR. KENNEDY. (*Cutting across him.*) Because it's not like it used to be, and it's never going to be that way again. See, the people you used to run out of town on a rail got them AR-15 semi-automatics with hollow-point ammunition, got them Ingrim Mach-10's hanging over their fireplaces equipped with infa-red pathfinder night-scopes, got them eight-ply bulletproof glass in their Mercedes Benzes, .45 pistols in quick-draw vest holsters and . . . (*Takes something round out of his coat pocket.*) when they go out to pick up the paper in the morning, they are carrying an unpinned double-ought-three fragmentation grenade in their free hand. Hey, what used to be lynch-bait is now 'Nam-trained, half-nasty, and armed to our glow-in-the-dark teeth. Now what I want you to understand is that I don't care to take your jobs, mutilate your bodies or steal your fraternal hand-

shake. I just want to pull your teeth in a general atmosphere of wary, mutual respect. It's either that, or it's this. (*Squeezes off a shot.*) And uh, listen up now, don't kid a kidder, O.K.? I am *trained* to hurt you. Got it? Now pick up your trash and get your Invisible Empire off my lawn.

RYMAN. I got you down in my book, Nigra.

DR. KENNEDY. You tell these boys you're in the F.B.I. yet, Ryman?

RYMAN. (*Petrified.*) I ain't in the F.B.I.!

DR. KENNEDY. That's not what you told me out at the quarry.

RYMAN. I never went out to the quarry with him!

PRITCHARD. I got you down in my book, Ryman. (*They are picking up the lawn. Ryman reaches for the shotgun.*)

TRAVIS. Hey . . .

DR. KENNEDY. (*Turning the gun on Ryman. He freezes.*) Huh-uh. Oh, and leave me that big ol' cross. My momma'd like that. Go on.

BOBBY JOE. Dr. Kennedy, I dropped me a human glass eye-ball somewhere on your lawn. Y'all better watch out it don't get throwed up by your lawn mower.

DR. KENNEDY. O.K., son. I like your sheet.

BOBBY JOE. Onliest one she had.

ZITS. (*Taking off his hood.*) Sir? I'm Officer Puckett, sir? We met earlier? Well, I have successfully infiltrated this here Klavern, sir.

DR. KENNEDY. You dance divinely, Officer Puckett.

ZITS. Yes sir. So anyway, sir, I'll be puttin' these boys right in my cruiser an' takin' 'em in to Hueytown, sir. No fuss, no muss, sir. You can count on me, sir.

DR. KENNEDY. Officer Puckett, in my experience there is only one thing, historically, a black man absolutely *cannot* count on and that is the Alabama State Police. However, I would enjoy hearing you call me sir one more time.

ZITS. Yes sir, sir. (*The churchbells begin striking twelve.*)

DR. KENNEDY. 'Night boys. (*They don't move.*) Time to get on home now. (*They don't move.*) Slow learners. (*He pulls the pin on the grenade he's been holding.*) Bye, bye. (*He lobs the grenade out into the assemblage.*)

TOOTH. Grenade! (*The Klansmen scatter offstage in every direction.*)

Only Travis stands stock still. The others are gone. Travis calmly picks up the grenade and tosses it back to Dr. Kennedy.)

TRAVIS. That ain't no live grenade. I was *there* buddy. I-26 Armored.

DR. KENNEDY. Special Forces. Junk Yard Dogs. Semi-detached.

TRAVIS. Sixty-six, sixty-seven.

DR. KENNEDY. Sixty-six, sixty-seven. (*In other words they both served the same years.*)

TRAVIS. You boys was O.K. . . .

DR. KENNEDY. (*He and Travis eye each other.*) I was looking at your card the other day. It's time for you to come in and get your teeth cleaned.

TRAVIS. Like to talk to my wife, if you don't mind.

DR. KENNEDY. Sounds like one hell of a good idea to me. Goodnight, Essie.

ESSIE. Goodnight, Harold.

DR. KENNEDY. You know, I knew a guy once came home and caught his wife layin' under their car with a strange man, high noon, in his own damn driveway. Shot off three toes on her left foot, and then found out later they were just fixing the muffler. (*Looks up.*) Hell of a nice night. (*Goes in and closes the door.*)

ESSIE. (*There is a pause. Travis looks at her. First he nods his head yes, then he shakes it no. He slaps his fist into his hand several times.*) You're gonna do it, aren't you? (*He omits a low growl, punctuated by hitting his own shoulders.*) Told me on New Years' you weren't gonna do it no more. (*He yells a bloodcurdling yell. He hits his chest with a closed fist. He pounds on his thighs. He throws a couple of wild punches into the air and then socks himself a good one in the jaw. It knocks him down. He is up immediately taking a barrage of blows. He switches to the midsection, grunting as he takes the punches. He gets down on his knees and pounds his head on the ground. Leaps up, emits a blood-curdling cry and throws himself out full length, hitting the ground. He rolls over on his back, grabs himself by the hair, and swats his head on the ground three times. Rises groggily to his knees and unleashes a final corker to his jaw. He lies full length on the ground.*) I've been married to you nineteen years, an' it's still the goddamnedest thing I've ever seen.

TRAVIS. Shoot! (*A rat-a-tat-tat of firecrackers in the distance.*)

ESSIE. People still shootin' off fireworks. Come sit on the curb with me.

TRAVIS. Boy, I tell you!

ESSIE. You're gonna be so sore. If I don't soak a flannel shirt in lard an' turpentine, you just won't be able to move a muscle tomorrow.

TRAVIS. (*Still prone.*) Who's with the damn kids?

ESSIE. Bitsy. Probably drinkin' our whiskey. Come on Travis, sit. You can beat me up later.

TRAVIS. (*Not moving.*) What the hell were you doin' in there?

ESSIE. Listenin' to music, talkin' about the parade . . .

TRAVIS. Parade! (*He hits himself, still lying down, several times, but not as hard as before.*)

ESSIE. Travis! Oh, an' he read some to me.

TRAVIS. Read to you what?

ESSIE. *Ko*ran.

TRAVIS. What the hell's that?

ESSIE. You hadn't shot up the place I mighta' found out.

TRAVIS. Whole damn Klavern saw you was in there.

ESSIE. After that dance they did, I don't think they'll tease you much. (*She laughs.*) Haven't seen those boys dance since Cotillion.

TRAVIS. (*Getting up.*) That Nigra touch you?

ESSIE. No, sir.

TRAVIS. You damn sure?

ESSIE. I'm damn sure.

TRAVIS. You swear on your children's heads, your dead momma's grave, Christ your savior, your bodily health an' Bear Bryant's hat?

ESSIE. He didn't touch me, Travis.

TRAVIS. What did he do?

ESSIE. Talked to me like a human being.

TRAVIS. I don't know, man. I was nineteen, they was all good days; got to be thirty, they was good days an' bad days; now I'm forty, an' it seems like I'm jes' alla time knee-deep in shit. I ain't got the hang of this thing no more.

ESSIE. Didn't teach us right.

TRAVIS. Yeah, maybe.

ESSIE. We started dumb, an' they taught us dumb, an' they kep' us dumb. Musta' been somethin' in it for 'em. (*A pause.*)

You still like me, Travis? (*He doesn't react.*) Well, you didn't say no. You ever think about the mystery of life?

TRAVIS. He didn't make you take no drugs, did he?

ESSIE. (*Shakes her head no.*) Some mornin's, when I'm scramblin' your brains an' eggs, jes' when I put the catsup on, I think, "This ain't it."

TRAVIS. Brings out the flavor.

ESSIE. No, this. (*Gestures at everything.*) This.

TRAVIS. (*Trying to follow her.*) You want me to put my own catsup on?

ESSIE. No, I . . . Travis . . . no, look, it's like . . . it's like when I read one a them Max Brand Westerns you got . . .

TRAVIS. "Flamin' Irons"?

ESSIE. Yeah, that one . . . an' it's a good story, an' there's a whole lot happenin' . . .

TRAVIS. It's the best one.

ESSIE. But there's not much . . . shoot, I don't know . . . not much . . .

DR. KENNEDY. (*From inside the house. He has been listening by a window.*) Content.

TRAVIS. (*Springs up.*) Goddamnit Kennedy, butt out! (*A venetian-blind tumbles down.*)

ESSIE. Travis . . .

TRAVIS. Go stuff a watermelon in yer big damn mouth!

ESSIE. Travis!

TRAVIS. (*A mountain of frustration.*) Flub-a-dub-a-dub-a-dub-a-dub.

ESSIE. Not enough content.

TRAVIS. Sittin' on a damn curb takin' thinkin' lessons from a Nigra.

ESSIE. Well, he's *on* it, don't you think? Must be somethin' better.

TRAVIS. Well hell, *that's* the dad-blamed, one hunnert percent, mother of pearl, everlovin' truth.

ESSIE. You know, Harold played me a real nice record.

TRAVIS. Essie, you're callin' a colored by his first name.

ESSIE. Yes. (*A pause.*) Second time you came courtin' you brought me stale candy an' sang "Scoundrels and Ramblers" *

---

* Music for this song appears at the back of playbook.

71

. . . played yer brother I.W.'s guitar . . . more or less. Haven't sung to me since.

TRAVIS. Well, I forgot "Ace's Wild."

ESSIE. Want to learn a new tune? Travis? Huh?

TRAVIS. What tune?

ESSIE. Do you?

TRAVIS. I'm listenin'.

ESSIE. Now it's real different.

TRAVIS. I said I was listenin'.

ESSIE. All right now, get ready. (*Sings him the final "Ode to Joy" phrase of Beethoven's Ninth.*) Do it.

TRAVIS. I cain't sing that.

ESSIE. You too dumb t' learn a new tune? (*She repeats the phrase.*) Come on. (*He tries it grudgingly.*) Not too raggedy. (*She does a second phrase.*)

TRAVIS. Aw, come on Essie. This is nigger music.

ESSIE. No, you come on. (*She does the second phrase again. He repeats it.*) You got it, Baby Blue. (*A yellow flashing two-truck beacon hits them from off.*)

TRAVIS. I cain't do this.

ESSIE. Come on, Travis. Yer learnin' some new tricks.

TRAVIS. (*Rising suddenly, looking off.*) Damn. Dumb.

ESSIE. You're *not* dumb.

TRAVIS. I *am* dumb! (*Hits himself in chest.*)

ESSIE. (*Furious.*) Why do you say that!

TRAVIS. 'Cause it's one a.m. an' there's a State Police tow-truck haulin' off m' Toyota fer bein' parked in a handicapped zone!

ESSIE. That is dumb!

TRAVIS. That's right! (*Hits himself.*)

ESSIE. You make me so damn mad! (*She hits herself.*)

TRAVIS. Hey. (*Essie hits herself again.*) Hey! (*Hits herself.*) Knock it off. (*Hits herself several times. He grabs her. She struggles. He makes her stop. He stands holding her for a moment.*)

ESSIE. I have to sit down. (*He releases her, she sits on curb. A heavy metal clonk is heard offstage.*) What was that?

TRAVIS. (*Looking off.*) Engine fell outta' my car. (*Flashing yellow light fades. He sits by her. Silence. She begins to sing softly.*)

ESSIE.

"Oh don't let yer daughters love dealers.

72

For they'll sell both their soul an' yer child.
Oh Riverboat gamblers,
They're scoundrels and ramblers,
Gone at dawn and their game's
Ace's wild."
(*She nudges him and he sings.*)
"Ace's wild, ace's wild, ain't no game fer yer child."
(*They both sing.*)
"Gone at dawn and their game's
Ace's wild."
(*They sit, silent. Firecrackers in distance. Lights fade.*)

BLACKOUT

PROPERTY LIST—"COUPS"

@ Southern Mansion—all white upholstery, all painted white wood on furniture

2 Sidechairs
2 Armchairs
1 Window Seat
1 Coffee height round marble top table
2 Wall Pier tables
2 Busts—Jefferson Davis
              Robert E. Lee
4 Sets full swag draperies
1 White floral arrangement in crystal bowl

Hairdresser equip.—Don S.
  hand mirror
  curling iron
  comb
  haircombs
  hairspray

Towel—Tooth

1 rubber tree plant in urn planter—Beulah
1 feather duster
Silver tray
  3 cups coffee
  Silver sugar bowl w. sugar cubes
  Silver creamer
Silver tray
  3 crystal bowls w. mixed nuts
Glass (for gin)
Candy dish w. lemon pastilles

Nail buffer
Bottle of gin
Straw hat

Waist cincher
Box of rags — should be app. 1' × 1' sq. rags, white
Can of crisco — empty crisco and fill with make-up remover
Lemon pastilles tin
Cake knife
Meat tenderizer — wooden and nonthreatening
Pistol — hidden in coffee table — not fired

Shredded shoe — Bobby Joe

PROPERTY LIST—"CLUCKS"

Airline Flight Bag—holds KKK robe
Coins—quarter
Sparkler—burned one nightly—should last at least 30 sec.
Matchbooks—1 empty
                1 full
Glass eye

Buck knife
½ pt. whiskey bottle

Magic marker
Bowl of popcorn
Police gun and holster—gun fired twice

Bag of almonds
Garbage bag—holds KKK robe
Plastic coin purse
Wooden cross wrapped in burlap—must withstand dropping
   nightly
Tool box
   w. dynamite sticks/clock/wires bomb
   screwdriver
   pliers
Gold plated pen
Bic lighter—broken nightly
Pistol in shoulder holster

Bic lighter—broken nightly
Joint
Twigs—broken nightly
Gob of melted M & M's
M & M's bag

Rubber—Royal Sultan Super Sensitive, Money back guarantee, Extra Small
Bucket of water

AR-15 Semi automatic—fires burst of gunshot
Hand grenade—pin should be pullable

4 sets curtains for wall backing—drk. grey—on traverse rods
2 planters around porch
3 exterior wall mount yard lights

COSTUME PLOT—"COUP"

Miz Zifty:

Merry widow
Camisole
Drawers
Scarlett dress
Sash *
Straw hat *
Green heels
Green slippers *
Wig

Brenda Lee:

Merry widow
Bloomers
Melanie dress
Fan
Grey heels
Pantyhose
Purse
Watch

Beulah:

Maid's uniform
Stockings
Black shoes
Glasses
Slip
Scarlett dress *
Sash *

NOTE: * Indicates change takes place during course of play.

Tooth:

Brown frock coat
Beige pants and vest
Brown cravat
Suspenders
Beige planter's hat
White formal shirt
Brown shoes
Socks
T-shirt with lettering
Red boxer shorts

Bobby Joe:

Jeans
Blue t-shirt
Sneakers
Socks
Shredded tennis shoe
Boxer shorts
Ashley suit *

Essie:

Mammy dress
Apron
Head and neck scarves
Slip
Pantyhose
Black shoes
India dress *
Orange heels
Snood

Dr. Kennedy:

Black faille suit
Grey vest
Brown cravat
Suspenders
Grey planter's hat

White formal shirt
Black oxfords
Black socks
Handkerchief

Don:

Magenta knit shirt
Purple check shirt
Grey slacks
Magenta socks
Grey shoes
Zoave silver vest *
Black jacket *
Striped pants *
Sash *
Turban *
Gaiters *
Black shoes *
Scarlett dress *
Blue undershirt
Briefs
Ashley suit *

COSTUME PLOT—"CLUCKS"

TRAVIS
Plaid shirt
Blue jeans
Boots
Socks
Belt
Klan robe with hood (with red lining)
Red sash

BOBBY JOE
Print boxer shorts
Sneakers
Violet print sheet robe with pillow case hood.

TOOTH
Brown coveralls
Workboots
Brown "Shell" cap

PRITCHARD
Thermal shirt
Overalls
Sneakers
Socks
Handkerchief
Red Klan robe with red hood
Red sash

RYMAN
Brown suit
Stripe shirt
Stripe tie
Brown belt
Wire rim glasses

Black shoes
Socks
Klan robe and hood (with green lining)
Green sash

DR. KENNEDY
Tan stripe shirt
Off-white jacket
Brown slacks
Brown knit tie
Shoes
Socks

ZITS
Trooper shirt
Trooper pants
Blue grey hat
Black belt
Holster belt with accessories
Tank undershirt
Black shoes
Socks
Klan pants and top with hood (Blue lined)
Blue sash

ESSIE
Lavender dress
Slip
Canvas sandals
Panty hose

Scoundrels and Ramblers

Lyrics: Jane Martin
Music: Daniel Jenkins

From "Clocks" by Jane Martin

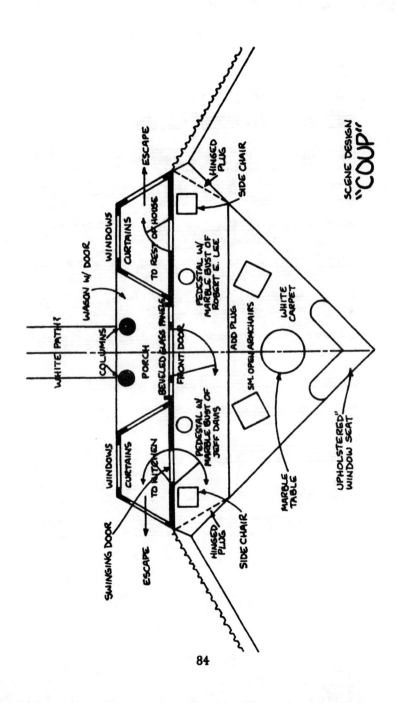

SCENE DESIGN "COUP"

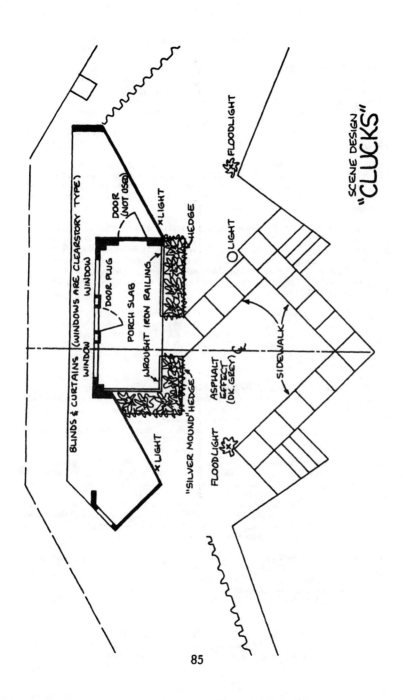

SCENE DESIGN
"CLUCKS"

BLINDS & CURTAINS (WINDOWS ARE CLEARSTORY TYPE)
WINDOW
WINDOW
DOOR (NOT USED)
DOOR PLUG
×LIGHT
PORCH SLAB
WROUGHT IRON RAILING
HEDGE
"SILVER MOUND" HEDGE
×LIGHT
ASPHALT EFFECT (DK. GREY)
○LIGHT
FLOODLIGHT
FLOODLIGHT
SIDEWALK

NEW PLAYS

★ **MONTHS ON END by Craig Pospisil.** In comic scenes, one for each month of the year, we follow the intertwined worlds of a circle of friends and family whose lives are poised between happiness and heartbreak. "...a triumph...these twelve vignettes all form crucial pieces in the eternal puzzle known as human relationships, an area in which the playwright displays an assured knowledge that spans deep sorrow to unbounded happiness." –*Ann Arbor News.* "...rings with emotional truth, humor...[an] endearing contemplation on love...entertaining and satisfying." –*Oakland Press.* [5M, 5W] ISBN: 0-8222-1892-5

★ **GOOD THING by Jessica Goldberg.** Brings us into the households of John and Nancy Roy, forty-something high-school guidance counselors whose marriage has been increasingly on the rocks and Dean and Mary, recent graduates struggling to make their way in life. "...a blend of gritty social drama, poetic humor and unsubtle existential contemplation..." –*Variety.* [3M, 3W] ISBN: 0-8222-1869-0

★ **THE DEAD EYE BOY by Angus MacLachlan.** Having fallen in love at their Narcotics Anonymous meeting, Billy and Shirley-Diane are striving to overcome the past together. But their relationship is complicated by the presence of Sorin, Shirley-Diane's fourteen-year-old son, a damaged reminder of her dark past. "...a grim, insightful portrait of an unmoored family..." –*NY Times.* "MacLachlan's play isn't for the squeamish, but then, tragic stories delivered at such an unrelenting fever pitch rarely are." –*Variety.* [1M, 1W, 1 boy] ISBN: 0-8222-1844-5

★ **[SIC] by Melissa James Gibson.** In adjacent apartments three young, ambitious neighbors come together to discuss, flirt, argue, share their dreams and plan their futures with unequal degrees of deep hopefulness and abject despair. "A work...concerned with the sound and power of language..." –*NY Times.* "...a wonderfully original take on urban friendship and the comedy of manners—a *Design for Living* for our times..." –*NY Observer.* [3M, 2W] ISBN: 0-8222-1872-0

★ **LOOKING FOR NORMAL by Jane Anderson.** Roy and Irma's twenty-five-year marriage is thrown into turmoil when Roy confesses that he is actually a woman trapped in a man's body, forcing the couple to wrestle with the meaning of their marriage and the delicate dynamics of family. "Jane Anderson's bittersweet transgender domestic comedy-drama ...is thoughtful and touching and full of wit and wisdom. A real audience pleaser." –*Hollywood Reporter.* [5M, 4W] ISBN: 0-8222-1857-7

★ **ENDPAPERS by Thomas McCormack.** The regal Joshua Maynard, the old and ailing head of a mid-sized, family-owned book-publishing house in New York City, must name a successor. One faction in the house backs a smart, "pragmatic" manager, the other faction a smart, "sensitive" editor and both factions fear what the other's man could do to this house— and to them. "If Kaufman and Hart had undertaken a comedy about the publishing business, they might have written *Endpapers*...a breathlessly fast, funny, and thoughtful comedy ...keeps you amused, guessing, and often surprised...profound in its empathy for the paradoxes of human nature." –*NY Magazine.* [7M, 4W] ISBN: 0-8222-1908-5

★ **THE PAVILION by Craig Wright.** By turns poetic and comic, romantic and philosophical, this play asks old lovers to face the consequences of difficult choices made long ago. "The script's greatest strength lies in the genuineness of its feeling." –*Houston Chronicle.* "Wright's perceptive, gently witty writing makes this familiar situation fresh and thoroughly involving." –*Philadelphia Inquirer.* [2M, 1W (flexible casting)] ISBN: 0-8222-1898-4

DRAMATISTS PLAY SERVICE, INC.
440 Park Avenue South, New York, NY 10016 212-683-8960 Fax 212-213-1539
postmaster@dramatists.com www.dramatists.com

NEW PLAYS

★ **BE AGGRESSIVE by Annie Weisman.** Vista Del Sol is paradise, sandy beaches, avocado-lined streets. But for seventeen-year-old cheerleader Laura, everything changes when her mother is killed in a car crash, and she embarks on a journey to the Spirit Institute of the South where she can learn "cheer" with Bible belt intensity. "...filled with lingual gymnastics...stylized rapid-fire dialogue..." –*Variety*. "...a new, exciting, and unique voice in the American theatre..." –*BackStage West*. [1M, 4W, extras] ISBN: 0-8222-1894-1

★ **FOUR by Christopher Shinn.** Four people struggle desperately to connect in this quiet, sophisticated, moving drama. "...smart, broken-hearted...Mr. Shinn has a precocious and forgiving sense of how power shifts in the game of sexual pursuit...He promises to be a playwright to reckon with..." –*NY Times*. "A voice emerges from an American place. It's got humor, sadness and a fresh and touching rhythm that tell of the loneliness and secrets of life...[a] poetic, haunting play." –*NY Post*. [3M, 1W] ISBN: 0-8222-1850-X

★ **WONDER OF THE WORLD by David Lindsay-Abaire.** A madcap picaresque involving Niagara Falls, a lonely tour-boat captain, a pair of bickering private detectives and a husband's dirty little secret. "Exceedingly whimsical and playfully wicked. Winning and genial. A top-drawer production." –*NY Times*. "Full frontal lunacy is on display. A most assuredly fresh and hilarious tragicomedy of marital discord run amok...absolutely hysterical..." –*Variety*. [3M, 4W (doubling)] ISBN: 0-8222-1863-1

★ **QED by Peter Parnell.** Nobel Prize-winning physicist and all-around genius Richard Feynman holds forth with captivating wit and wisdom in this fascinating biographical play that originally starred Alan Alda. "QED is a seductive mix of science, human affections, moral courage, and comic eccentricity. It reflects on, among other things, death, the absence of God, travel to an unexplored country, the pleasures of drumming, and the need to know and understand." –*NY Magazine*. "Its rhythms correspond to the way that people—even geniuses—approach and avoid highly emotional issues, and it portrays Feynman with affection and awe." –*The New Yorker*. [1M, 1W] ISBN: 0-8222-1924-7

★ **UNWRAP YOUR CANDY by Doug Wright.** Alternately chilling and hilarious, this deliciously macabre collection of four bedtime tales for adults is guaranteed to keep you awake for nights on end. "Engaging and intellectually satisfying...a treat to watch." –*NY Times*. "Fiendishly clever. Mordantly funny and chilling. Doug Wright teases, freezes and zaps us." –*Village Voice*. "Four bite-size plays that bite back." –*Variety*. [flexible casting] ISBN: 0-8222-1871-2

★ **FURTHER THAN THE FURTHEST THING by Zinnie Harris.** On a remote island in the middle of the Atlantic secrets are buried. When the outside world comes calling, the islanders find their world blown apart from the inside as well as beyond. "Harris winningly produces an intimate and poetic, as well as political, family saga." –*Independent (London)*. "Harris' enthralling adventure of a play marks a departure from stale, well-furrowed theatrical terrain." –*Evening Standard (London)*. [3M, 2W] ISBN: 0-8222-1874-7

★ **THE DESIGNATED MOURNER by Wallace Shawn.** The story of three people living in a country where what sort of books people like to read and how they choose to amuse themselves becomes both firmly personal and unexpectedly entangled with questions of survival. "This is a playwright who does not just tell you what it is like to be arrested at night by goons or to fall morally apart and become an aimless yet weirdly contented ghost yourself. He has the originality to make you feel it." –*Times (London)*. "A fascinating play with beautiful passages of writing..." –*Variety*. [2M, 1W] ISBN: 0-8222-1848-8

DRAMATISTS PLAY SERVICE, INC.
440 Park Avenue South, New York, NY 10016 212-683-8960 Fax 212-213-1539
postmaster@dramatists.com www.dramatists.com

NEW PLAYS

★ SHEL'S SHORTS by Shel Silverstein. Lauded poet, songwriter and author of children's books, the incomparable Shel Silverstein's short plays are deeply infused with the same wicked sense of humor that made him famous. "...[a] childlike honesty and twisted sense of humor." *–Boston Herald.* "...terse dialogue and an absurdity laced with a tang of dread give [*Shel's Shorts*] more than a trace of Samuel Beckett's comic existentialism." *–Boston Phoenix.* [flexible casting] ISBN: 0-8222-1897-6

★ AN ADULT EVENING OF SHEL SILVERSTEIN by Shel Silverstein. Welcome to the darkly comic world of Shel Silverstein, a world where nothing is as it seems and where the most innocent conversation can turn menacing in an instant. These ten imaginative plays vary widely in content, but the style is unmistakable. "...[*An Adult Evening*] shows off Silverstein's virtuosic gift for wordplay...[and] sends the audience out...with a clear appreciation of human nature as perverse and laughable." *–NY Times.* [flexible casting] ISBN: 0-8222-1873-9

★ WHERE'S MY MONEY? by John Patrick Shanley. A caustic and sardonic vivisection of the ¡ ˙azor-sharp wit. "...Shan￼ ￼nges is certainly potent...￼ ￼ wisdom." *–NY Times.* [￼

★ A FE￼ ￼crewy comedy-drama th￼ ￼urrounded by a cast of fa￼ ￼, the opera star Adelina ￼ ￼yrocket to awe-some hei￼ ￼t you might call an every￼ ￼ *ıge Voice.* [10M, 3W] ISE￼

★ BRE￼ ￼e life of Prix, a Bronx na￼ ￼oming to matu-rity at th￼ ￼a dramatic visit, where no￼ ￼ith humor, terse vernacular strength and gritty detail..." *–Variety.* [1M, 9W] ISBN: 0-8222-1849-6

★ THE LATE HENRY MOSS by Sam Shepard. Two antagonistic brothers, Ray and Earl, are brought together after their father, Henry Moss, is found dead in his seedy New Mexico home in this classic Shepard tale. "...His singular gift has been for building mysteries out of the ordinary ingredients of American family life..." *–NY Times.* "...rich moments ...Shepard finds gold." *–LA Times.* [7M, 1W] ISBN: 0-8222-1858-5

★ THE CARPETBAGGER'S CHILDREN by Horton Foote. One family's history span-ning from the Civil War to WWII is recounted by three sisters in evocative, intertwining monologues. "...bittersweet music—[a] rhapsody of ambivalence...in its modest, garrulous way...theatrically daring." *–The New Yorker.* [3W] ISBN: 0-8222-1843-7

★ THE NINA VARIATIONS by Steven Dietz. In this funny, fierce and heartbreaking homage to *The Seagull,* Dietz puts Chekhov's star-crossed lovers in a room and doesn't let them out. "A perfect little jewel of a play..." *–Shepherdstown Chronicle.* "...a delightful rev-elation of a writer at play; and also an odd, haunting, moving theater piece of lingering beauty." *–Eastside Journal (Seattle).* [1M, 1W (flexible casting)] ISBN: 0-8222-1891-7

DRAMATISTS PLAY SERVICE, INC.
440 Park Avenue South, New York, NY 10016 212-683-8960 Fax 212-213-1539
postmaster@dramatists.com www.dramatists.com